WHAT EVEN IS

Debates about gender are everywhere. Is it an inner identity, a biological fact, or an oppressive system? Should we respect it or resist it?

What Even Is Gender? shifts the conversation in a fresh direction, arguing that these debates rest on a shared mistake: the idea that there is one thing called "gender" that both sides are arguing about. The authors distinguish a range of phenomena that established vocabulary often lumps together. This sheds light on the equivocations and false dichotomies of "gender" talk and how they deny many of us the tools to make our needs, experiences, and concerns intelligible to others or even to ourselves.

The authors develop a conceptual toolkit that helps alleviate the harms that result from the limitations of familiar approaches. They propose a pluralistic concept of "gender feels" that distinguishes among our experiences of diverse facets of gendered life. They develop a flexible approach to gender categories that reflects the value of self-determination. And they suggest that what we need is not one universal language of gender but an awareness of individual variation and a willingness to adjust to changing contexts and circumstances.

A bold and thought-provoking approach to thinking about gender, *What Even Is Gender?* will be of great interest to those in philosophy, gender studies, sociology, and LGBTQIA+ studies.

R. A. Briggs is Professor of Philosophy at Stanford University, USA, and received their PhD in philosophy from MIT. Their interests include metaphysics, epistemology, and feminist philosophy, and their work has appeared in such journals as *The Philosophical Review*, *Philosophical Studies*, and *Noûs*. They also write poetry and co-host the weekly radio show *Philosophy Talk*.

B. R. George is a neurodivergent trans cyborg disaster bisexual residing in Pittsburgh, Pennsylvania, USA. Their work on topics like "What does that even mean?" and "Someone is wrong on the internet" has appeared in such journals as *Bioethics*, *Feminist Philosophy Quarterly*, *Natural Language Semantics*, and *Thought*.

WHAT EVEN IS GENDER?

R. A. Briggs and B. R. George

Routledge
Taylor & Francis Group
LONDON AND NEW YORK

Cover image: Pok Man Ip / Getty Images

First published 2023
by Routledge
4 Park Square, Milton Park, Abingdon, Oxon OX14 4RN

and by Routledge
605 Third Avenue, New York, NY 10158

Routledge is an imprint of the Taylor & Francis Group, an informa business

British Library Cataloguing-in-Publication Data
A catalogue record for this book is available from the British
Library

Library of Congress Cataloging-in-Publication Data
A catalog record has been requested for this book

ISBN: 978-0-367-51317-7 (hbk)
ISBN: 978-0-367-51321-4 (pbk)
ISBN: 978-1-003-05333-0 (ebk)

DOI: 10.4324/9781003053330

Typeset in Bembo
by Apex CoVantage, LLC

For everyone who's ever been told they were impossible

CONTENTS

Acknowledgments   *viii*

1   Introduction   1

2   All The Feels: Against "Gender Identity"   19

3   Don't Hate the Player: Traits Versus Norms   64

4   "Above All That": Glorifying Indifference   100

5   Our Princess Is in Another Castle: There
    Is No Essence of Womanhood   131

6   Conclusion   175

Index   *181*

ACKNOWLEDGMENTS

This book has benefited from the generosity of many people who were willing to devote their time and attention to helping us refine our ideas and present them more clearly.

Thanks to the audiences who attended our talks at Stanford, Carnegie Mellon University, Dartmouth, MIT, the University of Pittsburgh, the University of Birmingham, the Central APA, MANCEPT, the Universitat de Barcelona, the University of Illinois Chicago, UW Madison, and The National University of Singapore. You provided invaluable opportunities to talk through our ideas with other philosophers, and we appreciate your insightful questions and comments.

Thanks to Matt Andler, Louise Antony, Rowan Bell, Sharon Berry, Lisa Brush, Arthur Chu, Jessica Collins, Graeme Forbes, Jason Grossman, Leif Hancox-Li, Samantha Hancox-Li, Jas Heaton, Os Keyes, Nico Orlandi, Dee Payton, Anya Plutynski, David Ripley, Luke Roelofs, Sarita Rosenstock, and Alexandrin Zuser, and everyone else who attended the reading group in which we developed the manuscript, and to Marley Alexander, Erika R. Alpert, Jules Bertaut, Talia Mae Bettcher, Liam Kofi Bright, Tova Brown, Sam Crane, Helen Daly, Jorah Dannenberg, Fox Darby, Tom Davies, Rax E. Dillon, Lila Garrot, Stacey Goguen, Carrie Ichikawa Jenkins, Lucian Kahn, Quill Kukla, Rebecca Mason, Elin McCready, Jack Parker, Elliot Reed,

Chelsea Rosenthal, Rachel Sapiro, Skuld, Scott Sturgeon, Bobbi Tables, Alex Temple, Giuliano Torrengo, Jennifer Wang, and Danielle M. Wenner, among others, for other conversations and feedback that contributed to the development of this project.

Thanks to Brian Earp, Naomi Scheman, and an anonymous referee, all of whom provided detailed, helpful, and charitable comments on our first draft of this manuscript. You are not to blame for any remaining errors or oversights, but you deserve a great deal of credit for the fact that there are not more of them.

From Ray: Thanks to Brent Barker, Blossom Briggs, Oliver Hahn, Quinn McKissock, Sofia Maystrenko, and Jess White for your invaluable moral and immoral support. Without you, I might have languished and perished before the book was complete.

From B: Thanks to the various family, friends, and lovers who have been sources of support and inspiration as this project has taken shape and to my trans friends on LiveJournal back in the day, who treated me with vastly more patience and empathy than I deserved.

1

INTRODUCTION

1.1 "What Is Gender?"

We might as well get the awkward part out of the way: despite the title *What Even Is Gender?*, we're not going to tell you what "gender" is because this is a book built around the idea that "what is gender?" is the wrong question.

For both of us as trans people, the problems of "gender" are urgent practical problems and not (just) sources of abstract philosophical frustration. In this cultural moment, as scholars, pundits, and politicians debate "the transgender question", it seems like "gender" is everywhere. And we hear, again and again, that the legitimacy of our needs, and possibly our legitimacy as persons, depends upon a particular account of the metaphysics of "gender". We are told that we are a product of a dangerous "gender ideology", and many of our most influential enemies insist that they are justifiably "gender critical", so they simply cannot respect us, our rights, and our ways of existing.[1]

All of this is to say that there is considerable political urgency to the question of just what sort of "gender" (if any) might merit such a critical perspective and whether it has anything to do with us as trans people, with our continued existence in our society, or with the political demands of trans liberation.

DOI: 10.4324/9781003053330-1

As can be seen throughout this book, we think that there is a lot that merits criticism in the ways that we talk about "gender", whether in feminist theory, in mainstream political debate, or in well-intentioned "trans 101" resources. But we also think that we don't *need* anything like the standard notion of "gender". In fact, we think that this notion – and the stories that come with it – often hurts more than it helps. Prevailing ways of talking about "gender" have many problems, but for us the most urgent is the way that they render many kinds of trans and gender-nonconforming experiences unintelligible, both to the wider society and to individual trans and gender-nonconforming people trying to make sense of our own lives.

On a more abstract philosophical level, our central thesis is that "What is gender?" is the wrong question because there is no one thing that answers to the name "gender" (or, for that matter, to the name "gender identity"). One major purpose of this book will be to identify some of the different things that "gender" talk is often gesturing at, to suggest an approach to distinguishing among them, and to show how conflating them under a single heading does real harm.

But before we can start to do the work of fleshing out these views, we need to provide some background and some clarification.

1.2 Who We Are and Who We're Writing For

This is a book about "gender" and some of its problems, written by two of its problems (more specifically, two nonbinary trans people). It is, in an important sense, written for our past selves.[2] It is a product of years of deeply felt confusion and frustration, produced by our experience of trying (and often failing) to make sense of "gender" discourse and to find ourselves within its stories and conceptual frameworks. We've tried to write a book that would have been useful to us, and that would have saved us from a certain amount of pain and regret, with the hope that we may, in some limited way, contribute to the shaping of a discursive environment in which others will not have to go through what we went through.

In light of this, it is unsurprising that our target audience is composed of people whose perspective bears some resemblance to our perspectives in various past life stages. If you are in the sort of place that we were once in – wondering "am I trans?" or "why doesn't this 'gender' talk make more logical sense?" – we hope this book will be useful to you.

In a bit more detail, this book is for two (overlapping) groups of readers. First, it's for people who have trouble reconciling their own gendered experiences with conversations about "gender" that they may have encountered, including (but not limited to) conversations in which everyone is presumed to have a clearly delineated "gender identity" which is readily accessible by intuition or in which "gender" seems to be understood entirely in individual, subjective, more-or-less internal terms or entirely in more-or-less external societal terms.

Second, it's for people who, while broadly sympathetic (or at least open) to the goals of trans inclusion and trans liberation, harbor some unease regarding the conceptual tensions, apparent contradictions, and metaphysical vagaries of the dominant rhetoric of trans politics. This sort of reader might feel the pull of some of the foundational concerns that they see raised in "gender critical" arguments, but is also trying to take their trans friends' anxious reactions seriously, and is loath to accept the political agenda that accompanies such arguments. If you do not feel especially threatened by the immediate practical implications of contemporary trans politics, but still harbor an uncomfortable feeling that something about their foundations doesn't quite make sense, then this is very much a book for you.

(It's also important to note something about who this book *isn't* for: if you see yourself as part of the "other side" of the "transgender debate", or cannot imagine a trans-centric book on "gender" having value except as a refutation of that "other side", then you are probably not in our target audience. We hope that you will find some of what we have to say illuminating, but we are not trying to meet you where you are.)

There are many ways in which a given reader may be unlike us. We are two white, anglophone philosophers based in the United States (one of us disabled), and our writing is, unavoidably, inflected with these features of our perspective. While we have tried to proceed with an awareness of these biases and limitations, and to be attentive to the ways in which the gender system interacts with race, ability, geography, language, and class, there is much work to be done in extending the ideas of this book beyond our own context and in exploring the diversity of these interactions. Our approach also unapologetically centers trans, queer, and gender-nonconforming experiences and perspectives, although we have tried not to assume this sort of firsthand experience on the part of our readers.[3]

Our audience is also varied in its background and assumptions. When sharing early drafts of this manuscript with friends and colleagues, we often observed stark differences in their perspectives. Some were shocked that we disputed the received understanding of gender identity (isn't that a theory that trans people are supposed to like?!); others thought our criticisms were so obvious that they hardly deserved the ink or the pixels we spilled. Some of our readers urged us to pay closer attention to the customary distinction between "sex" and "gender"; others complained that we seemed to presuppose a sex–gender distinction that they deemed outmoded and bogus.

We've done our best to avoid *needlessly* controversial assumptions, and to balance the competing demands of drawing on trans perspectives, making use of the insights of contemporary philosophy, and keeping the book reasonably accessible to readers who may be new to some of the subject matter. We've tried to paraphrase or explain many potentially unfamiliar terms in the text or in footnotes, and to make our assumptions explicit.[4] But we've opted not to spend too much time defending our terms and assumptions, including those that are more aligned with the approaches of some trans communities than with mainstream narratives about gender (or, for that matter, mainstream analytic philosophy). So while we're happy to explain that we use the adjective "cis" for anyone who is not trans, we aren't interested in giving a sharp set of criteria for distinguishing between cis and trans people or in arguing about whether "cis" is a slur.

Regardless of where you're coming from, if you are trying to make sense of your own relationship with one or more of the things called "gender", we hope this will help you to look beyond stock narratives about gendered life (cis or trans). While this book does not aim to refute anti-trans positions, we hope that even more skeptical readers will get *something* out of it – that they will feel inspired to view trans political demands and trans experience in a more charitable light, to engage with other work in this area, and to begin to examine and reevaluate parts of their own perspectives. Whoever you are, we hope this book can help you in some way to shape a gendered (or relatively ungendered) life that works for you.

1.3 What "Gender" Is Supposed to Be

Debates in feminism and trans politics are often framed in terms of a background assumption that "gender" names some particular thing and that the important questions and disagreements are concerned with what it truly is, where it comes from, or whether it is good or bad. In this book, we'll argue that questions posed in these terms are usually confused. "Gender" doesn't pick out any one thing; it equivocates among many. We'll develop a new framework with greater resources to distinguish among the candidate meanings of "gender".

To illustrate the problem better, let's consider some oft-repeated claims about what "gender" is:[5]

   Problematic Slogan 1: Gender is the social interpretation of sex.
   Problematic Slogan 2: Gender is an oppressive system that ties certain behaviors and characteristics to sex.
   Problematic Slogan 3: Gender is a performance of the role prescribed for one's sex.
   Problematic Slogan 4: Sex is *female*, *male*, etc.; gender is *feminine*, *masculine*, etc.
   Problematic Slogan 5: Sex is *female*, *male*, etc.; gender is *woman*, *man*, etc.

Alongside these claims about what "gender" *is*, in debates about trans life and trans experience we often encounter claims about what "gender" is *like*:

   Problematic Slogan 6: Gender is between your ears, not between your legs.
   Problematic Slogan 7: In transsexualism, biological sex conflicts with psychological gender.
   Problematic Slogan 8: A person is cisgender if and only if they identify with the gender they were assigned at birth.
   Problematic Slogan 9: Gender is an important, deeply felt aspect of the self, which deserves our respect.

We plan to argue that serious problems arise when we understand all these slogans as claims about one and the same thing, but, to start, let's note that each of them is getting at something worth talking about. Some of them are unnervingly vague, some of them incorporate debatable assumptions or political positions, and some use dated or offensive language, but, in their various more or less clumsy ways, they are all gesturing at important phenomena that deserve our attention.

Problematic Slogans 1–5 are all concerned with contrasting "gender" and "sex". The notion of "sex" is understood in many different ways, and it, the associated notion of distinct "sexes", and the "sex"/"gender" distinction all present their own difficulties. Still, whatever one thinks of these issues, there is clearly something important in this conceptual vicinity: humans have various physical characteristics that have traditionally been recognized as "sex" characteristics, which are important parts of human material reality and human experience. These are invested with various kinds of social significance (Problematic Slogan 1), much of it by way of a coercive power structure (Problematic Slogan 2), which prescribes different behaviors to different people (Problematic Slogans 3 and 4). There is ample reason to want to talk both about the power structure and about the specific behaviors that it prescribes. Problematic Slogan 5, meanwhile, directs our attention toward a certain sort of social categories that seem to be entangled in these power structures.

Problematic Slogans 6–9 emphasize the importance of subjective experience. Many people feel a strong sense of themselves as women or men (or both or neither), are drawn toward some "gendered" behaviors but not others, or have strong preferences about how they'd like their bodies' "sex" characteristics. These experiences are not fully determined by anatomy, as Problematic Slogan 6 points out. They can motivate trans people to alter our bodies, as Problematic Slogan 7 suggests, and can occur in cis as well as trans people, as Problematic Slogan 8 suggests. And they often hold deep personal significance, as Problematic Slogan 9 suggests.

The Problematic Slogans point us toward a bunch of conceptually *different* things, which the terminology invites us to regard as one thing – "gender". This immediately runs us into trouble. To pick an easy example, there exist people who are universally (or almost-universally) regarded as masculine women and feminine men, which seems to set Problematic Slogans 4 and 5 at odds. Some Problematic Slogans (like 2) treat "gender" *as a system*; others (like 9) treat it *as something specific to individuals* – how can it be both? Two people might have the same "gender" in the sense of Problematic Slogan 7 – seeking out the same medical interventions and aiming for the same physical outcomes – but different "genders" in the sense of Problematic Slogan 5 – perhaps one considers herself a woman while the other considers themself nonbinary.

The dominant language pushes us to explain how all these slogans can be true of the same thing, or else to wade into a debate about which of them captures what "gender" *really* is, presenting them as conflicting views of one thing. If we think that these slogans point at different topics, all of them worth discussing, then neither option is appealing. The former option makes "gender" into a conceptual monstrosity that is at best unwieldy and at worst incoherent, the latter option presents a forced choice among notionally distinct topics that are all worth discussing, and both are implicated in real harms to trans and gender-nonconforming people.

In what follows, we will explore some of the ways that the prevailing approach involving a catch-all notion of "gender" renders important areas of life more or less *unintelligible*. This unintelligibility makes it harder to reason and communicate about important aspects of our own subjectivity, as well as important social problems. That is, this is not just a matter of persnickety frustration with the imprecision of human language: to draw on a key insight of feminist social epistemology, *unintelligible is dangerous*.

1.4 Dangers of Gender Confusion

Why is it dangerous for trans people to be unintelligible? Shouldn't it be enough that we're left alone to do as we please? Must we demand *understanding* as well? But people who are rendered sufficiently unintelligible by their society are in severe danger of *not* being left alone to do as they please.

The standard conceptual toolkit for talking and thinking about "gender" enacts what social epistemologists call a *hermeneutical injustice* against trans people (Fricker, 2007; Medina, 2017); that is, it unfairly impairs society's ability to make meaning out of trans lives. The standard toolkit also creates a *hostile epistemic environment*, both in Nguyen's (2021) sense that it poses hazards that disrupt our ability to achieve knowledge and understanding (of trans lives in particular) and in the sense that the false beliefs themselves are hazards that disrupt our ability to live trans lives.

The problem is not just that a few individuals harbor overt transphobic prejudices but that our culture makes it easy for those prejudices to take hold and propagate, covertly embeds them in attempts to help trans people, and saddles us with internalized biases that we must overcome in order to make sense of our own lives. Someone who cannot imagine trans people's inner lives is more likely to imagine us as mad,[6] malicious, or monstrous. Someone with confused ideas about gender is more likely to be swayed by transphobic propaganda, even if they harbor no personal animosity toward trans people, perhaps without even recognizing this propaganda as transphobic. And a trans person who is hampered by inadequate expressive resources is less able to be an effective advocate for their own point of view.

The confusions that contribute to this hostile epistemic environment take a variety of forms. Many of these trace back to the ambiguity of "gender", which can lead people to see conflicts where none exist. For instance, by presenting Problematic Slogan 2 ("Gender is an oppressive system that ties certain behaviors and characteristics to sex") as a feminist slogan, and Problematic Slogan 9 ("Gender is an important, deeply felt aspect of the self, which deserves our respect") as a trans slogan, it is easy to create the appearance of conflict between "feminist" and "trans" views of what "gender" *really* is and so between "feminist" and "trans" agendas. Unsurprisingly, conservatives are all too happy to exploit this apparent conflict for their own ends (see Burns,

2019 for an in-depth discussion of ties between the anti-trans Women's Liberation Front and conservative anti-gay and anti-abortion groups).[7]

The ambiguity of "gender" can lead to other forms of confusion. People may accept multiple claims about "gender" that are (at least approximately) true of different things and improperly bring them together as premises in a single line of reasoning. Recall Problematic Slogans 7 ("In transsexualism, biological sex conflicts with psychological gender"), 3 ("Gender is a performance of the role prescribed for one's sex"), and 4 ("Sex is *female*, *male*, etc.; gender is *feminine*, *masculine*, etc."). Putting these claims together, one might conclude that whether someone counts as "transsexual" (and so has a legitimate "gender"-based reason to alter their biology) depends mainly on how well they perform stereotypically feminine or masculine behaviors. As we'll discuss in Chapter 2, this sort of thinking underlies some bizarre barriers for trans people seeking medical transition care.

To pick another example, consider a "gender critical" person who provisionally grants the definition of "cisgender" in Problematic Slogan 8 ("A person is cisgender if and only if they identify with the gender they were assigned at birth") but who then combines this Problematic Slogans 2 ("Gender is an oppressive system that ties certain behaviors and characteristics to sex") and 3 ("Gender is a performance of the role prescribed for one's sex"). Combining these claims, the person insists that to call a woman cisgender is to say that she identifies with her own oppression.[8]

Finally, the ambiguity of "gender" means that some questions about "gender" get disproportionate attention, metaphorically sucking up all the oxygen in the room, while others are ignored altogether. Too often, philosophers treat "what is gender?" as equivalent to "what is the nature of the categories *woman* and *man*?" or "who counts as a woman or a man?" (c.f. Problematic Slogan 5: "Sex is *female*, *male*, etc.; gender is *woman*, *man*, etc.")

while ignoring other complex social and psychological phenomena that go by the name of "gender".

In addition to equivocations, our hostile epistemic environment contains hidden assumptions, presupposed as part of the
conversational common ground,[9] that make it harder for cis people to understand trans people's points of view. These assumptions typically do not entail that trans people are lacking in any
way or that we deserve poor treatment. They are often embraced
by allies as well as enemies of trans people. But they set the terms
of the debate in ways that disadvantage trans perspectives.

An example of such a hidden assumption is that trans people's lives and feelings need to be legitimated by a metaphysically strong concept of "gender identity": one that is innate,
luminous to introspection, and unified. Defenders of trans rights
often attempt to make their case by establishing that such a thing
exists, while their opponents argue vehemently that it does not.
Treating the coherence of "gender identity" as a requirement
on trans legitimacy sets the terms of the debate in a way that
disadvantages trans people. (Cis people do not need to establish
analogous claims to be treated as members of their identified
gender or to access gender-affirming medical interventions.)[10]

These impoverished epistemic resources set limits on the
imagination. Cis people may be unable to imagine why anyone would medically or socially transition without an ulterior
motive (a strange sexual fetish,[11] perhaps, or an ambition so deep
it can only be slaked by male privilege, or a fixation on winning
women's sports trophies whatever the cost, or a hipsterish desire
to escape the drab mainstream fashion of being cis). Some closeted trans people (or those who would consider themselves trans
under more favorable conditions) may be unable to imagine the
possibility of transition because they fail to fit into a narrow and
sometimes contradictory set of expectations about what transition means. Any of us may have trouble imagining what it would
be like to relate to the various gendered aspects of our lives in a
way that does not rely on stereotypes.

We've noted that a hostile epistemic environment can have serious political consequences in the form of medical gatekeeping and transphobic political advocacy. The psychological burden of such an environment is also significant. Trans people may be led to doubt our own legitimacy ("how can I be trans if I don't match the cultural descriptions of trans people I've seen?") and to gatekeep each other's legitimacy ("I'm taking hormones; how can you be trans if you don't want hormones too?"), and unintelligibility is stressful and alienating even when it's not causing urgent practical problems.

While our book centers the perspectives and interests of trans people, we believe that many cis people can also benefit from cleaning up our shared epistemic resources. Some people who question their "gender" (in one or more senses of the word) ultimately decide not to transition. In a world with conceptual resources that make it easier to think things through, and imaginative resources that make it easier to picture the possibilities, this process would be smoother and less stressful regardless of the outcome. Many transphobic versions of feminism are also hostile to stereotypically feminine behaviors and choices, for reasons that are linked to the underlying confusions of "gender" talk.[12] We hope that the tools we provide will prove useful in efforts to critique this type of femmephobia.[13] And of course, the ability to form clear beliefs and envision alternative possibilities and life paths is intrinsically valuable for everyone, regardless of their own gender history.

1.5 What This Book Isn't

There are lots of things one might expect a book about gender to do – especially a book that centers contemporary problems of trans experience – and our book won't do them all. It won't directly address policy questions about how trans people should be treated in gendered sports or provide a systematic proposal when and under what circumstances trans minors should be able to access hormone replacement. Nor will it provide criteria for who should count as a woman, a man, nonbinary, trans, cis, etc.; in fact, we view such criteria with suspicion. Nor is it meant to be a complete theory of how sexist and transphobic oppression work.

More broadly, this book is not intended as a contribution to "the transgender debate". We won't refute popular transphobic or trans-exclusionary claims from first principles or systematically justify the various positions that have become associated with trans politics. At several points in the book, we will make trans-inclusive assumptions that the perceived "other side" of the "debate" will likely regard as question-begging. Our aim is to expose and critique the logic of the dominant way of thinking and speaking about gender, and to develop and advocate for new ways of framing these issues, from within a transfeminist perspective.[14]

This book is also not a "trans 101" primer, in at least two respects. First, it assumes prior familiarity with the sorts of topics covered in a typical "trans 101", primer and with the surrounding conversation. Second, it does not strive to represent something approximating a default or consensus picture of transness. Although we think that our views are broadly consistent with the norms of many trans-inclusive communities and with the project of trans liberation, the conceptual framework that we will be developing is novel and is the product of our profound dissatisfaction with the default conceptual framework of a typical "trans 101" presentation.

1.6 What This Book Is

The main goal of this book is to explore the assumptions and omissions of the dominant ways of talking about gender from a perspective of trans and gender-nonconforming experience and to present some pieces of an alternative interpretive framework that centers the insights and demands of such a perspective.

In the next two chapters, we'll introduce a conceptual framework that distinguishes many of the things that are often conflated under the rubric of "gender". We refer to this interrelated constellation of things as "the sex/gender system".

As its name suggests, the sex/gender system includes things discussed under the heading "(biological) sex", which some theorists (and some popular definitions) distinguish from gender. It also includes topics sometimes discussed under headings like "gender identity", "gender expression", and "gender role". We try to learn from the successes and failures of all of these concepts, but our approach to dividing up this conceptual space does not assume any of them and does not precisely reproduce any of them. In approaching things this way, we're implicitly challenging versions of the classic "sex"/"gender" distinction on which sex is a natural biological category, and gender is an artificial social structure built on top of it. We of course accept that there are biological traits like hormones, chromosomes, gametes, and so on, which are assigned various kinds of gendered significance, and we discuss them as a particular kind of material phenomenon belonging to the overarching sex/gender system.

Chapter 2 focuses on the subjective side of gender, particularly on phenomena that go by the name of "gender identity". We argue that the concept of "gender identity" is itself an unhelpful oversimplification and propose a more multifaceted replacement in terms of what we call "gender feels". Chapter 2 also introduces vocabulary for some of the outer trappings of gender: gender categories like *woman*, *man*, and *nonbinary*, sexed biology, and gendered behaviors. Gender feels are a certain kind of inner attitudes about one's relationship with these outward phenomena, and classifying them in terms of these phenomena proves useful throughout the book.

Chapter 3 shifts our attention to a more public aspect of the gender system: the social norms that link gender categories, sexed biology, and gendered behavior to one another. We consider *gender abolitionism*, the view that we should do away with gender altogether. Many gendered social norms are pernicious, and insofar as gender abolition targets them, it's a reasonable project. But "gender" means many things, so the target of "gender abolitionism" is not always clear. Chapter 3 criticizes the way that some gender abolitionists have shifted their attention from gender norms, many of which are legitimate targets of an abolitionist project, to the gendered behaviors and gender categories that the norms are about.

Chapter 4 returns to gender feels. Calling them "feels" evokes mainstream dismissals of trans subjectivity, but in Chapter 4, we argue that the correct response to gender feels is to *take them seriously*. Taking gender feels seriously means trusting one another's self-reports about gender feels, even when those self-reports don't match our own subjective responses to gendered phenomena. It also means assuming that others have good reasons for their gender feels: we should avoid treating reports of gender feels as born of confusion, or as cynical attempts to manipulate the sex/gender system for their own material advantage. We should take gender feels seriously not because they are *gender* feels, but because there we should take each other's subjectivity seriously by default, in general. We consider common reasons for overriding this default presupposition in the case of trans people's gender feels and find them wanting.

Chapter 5 develops a theory of gender categories motivated by a political value we call *gender self-determination*, which says that we should categorize people according to their expressed wishes rather than according to our own presuppositions or projections. Gender self-determination requires us to treat gender categories as *irreducible* in a certain sense: whether we classify someone as a man, a woman, a nonbinary, etc. cannot be settled by their sexed biological features, their gendered behaviors, their feels about sexed biological features and gendered behaviors, or the norms that a cissexist[15] society subjects them to. This irreducibility is sometimes thought to pose a metaphysical or conceptual problem and to make gender categories mysterious or viciously circular. We argue that there is no circularity problem for irreducible gender categories, and we sketch a positive theory of what such categories might be like.

Chapter 6 offers some brief concluding remarks.

Notes

1 As should surprise almost nobody, while trans people are frequently asked to justify our "gender" in order to legitimize our needs and decisions, those whose gendered lives conform to the societal mainstream are seldom asked to provide such justifications.

2 Other queers write young-adult fiction for their past selves, but we're philosophers, so this is what you're getting.

3 We have assumed a certain amount of passive cultural literacy on these topics. This book is not prepared to be your token queer friend.

4 We also have faith in your ability to look things up in cases where we have not provided such explanations or where you want more detail than we can provide in a short footnote.

5 These are simplified or idealized versions of positions on "gender" frequently seen in the wild, which we've attempted to paraphrase in a way that captures some of the tone, style, and presuppositions with which these views are usually articulated. You may have encountered some of these views in blog posts or op-ed pieces, in the feminist or sexological literature, in the slides or handouts at diversity and inclusion trainings, or on t-shirts or tote bags. Versions of most of the slogans can be found in the *Stanford Encyclopedia of Philosophy* entry on Feminist Perspectives on Sex and Gender (Mikkola, 2019), and in the chapters that follow, we'll discuss authors who endorse versions of a number of these views.

6 Not that we're all right with a society that treats mad people as unintelligible monsters!

7 These false conflicts have made their way into philosophy; just consider the 2020 PhilPapers survey question that asks respondents whether gender is biological, psychological, or social, as though there were a single phenomenon, "gender", that could be only one of these things (Bourget & Chalmers, 2021).

8 We have no great interest in describing any individual as "cisgender" if the term doesn't speak to them personally, but the claims described earlier are simply inconsistent with the observed semantics and usage of this term in discursive spaces where it is common.

9 Conversational common ground is, more or less, shared information that is taken for granted by all participants in a conversation. Stalnaker (2002) offers a formal characterization of common ground in terms of acceptance and belief, but nothing we say here turns on the details of that characterization.

10 Examples of gender-affirming medical interventions for cisgender people include, for example, gynecomastia surgery and treatment of certain hormone "deficits" or "imbalances". Cf. (Brown, 2022).

11 We don't think there's any problem with strange sexual fetishes, but we don't think much of a model that gives them a central place in the etiology of transness.

12 One common femmephobic argument moves from Problematic Slogan 2 ("Gender is an oppressive system that ties certain behaviors and characteristics to sex") and Problematic Slogan 4 ("Sex is *female*, *male*, etc.; gender is *feminine*, *masculine*, etc.") to the conclusion that feminine behavior is, by its nature, an endorsement of an oppressive system that ties certain behaviors and characteristics to sex.

13 We recognize that this is not the only reason that one might harbor feminist suspicion of various aspects of traditional femininity, but ruling out a current line of popular thought behind an especially sweeping femmephobic stance is still an important step toward clarifying the situation.

14 Books about phenomena like sexism or racism provide a helpful point of comparison. Some books concern themselves with refuting popular sexist or racist positions, persuading the reader that patriarchy and white supremacy exist, or converting sexist or racist readers into committed social justice activists. But others start by presupposing that sexism and racism are wrong and go on to describe and diagnose the workings of patriarchy or white supremacy, expose their scope and social pervasiveness, and propose alternatives to dominant sexist and racist scripts. What we're doing is more in line with the second type of project: we take a trans liberationist perspective as a point of departure and reasons from within that perspective.

15 We take the term "cissexist" from Serano (2007, p. 12), who defines "cissexism" as "the belief that transsexuals' identified genders are inferior to, or less authentic than, those of cissexuals". Even if we have reason to nitpick the vocabulary of "identified genders", Serano's intended meaning is intuitively clear, and she cites some illustrative examples: "misuse of pronouns or insisting the trans person use a different public restroom".

References

Bourget, D., & Chalmers, D. (2021). *Philosophers on philosophy: The 2020 PhilPapers survey*. https://survey2020.philpeople.org

Brown, J. T. (2022, October 30). When I started growing breasts as a teen boy, I got gender-affirming care without stigma. *NBC News*. www.nbcnews.com/think/opinion/gender-affirming-care-isnt-just-for-trans-people-rcna54651

Burns, K. (2019, September 5). The rise of anti-trans "radical" feminists, explained. *Vox*. www.vox.com/identities/2019/9/5/20840101/terfs-radical-feminists-gender-critical

Fricker, M. (2007). *Epistemic injustice: Power and the ethics of knowing*. Oxford University Press.

Medina, J. (2017). Varieties of hermeneutical injustice. In *The Routledge handbook of epistemic injustice* (pp. 41–52). Routledge.

Mikkola, M. (2019). Feminist perspectives on sex and gender. In *Stanford encyclopedia of philosophy*. https://plato.stanford.edu/entries/feminism-gender/

Nguyen, C. T. (2021). The seductions of clarity. *Royal Institute of Philosophy Supplements*, *89*, 227–255. https://doi.org/10.1017/S1358246121000035

Serano, J. (2007). *Whipping girl: A transsexual woman on sexism and the scapegoating of femininity*. Seal Press.

Stalnaker, R. (2002). Common ground. *Linguistics and Philosophy*, *25*(5–6), 701–721. https://doi.org/10.1023/a:1020867916902

2

ALL THE FEELS

Against "Gender Identity"

2.1 The Trouble With "Gender Identity"

Gender identity is typically understood as a deeply felt inner sense of one's gender.[1] In this chapter, we argue that the concept of "gender identity" is dangerously overburdened. It is expected to fill a variety of roles: justifying medical transition, explaining why people are drawn toward particular gendered behaviors as forms of self-expression, explaining why people like to be categorized as men or women or both or neither, and undergirding legitimacy of trans people's inner lives. While there is something that fills each of these roles, there is no one thing that fills them all. We develop an alternative conceptual toolkit that identifies different things that collectively do the work that "gender identity" is trying to do.

As we will explain in this chapter, the received narrative is not merely confusing; it causes real social and political harm. It prevents trans people from accessing hormones and surgeries unless we perform stereotypical behaviors to indicate our "gender identity". It enables trans-antagonistic writers to portray us as brainwashed dupes who see transition as the only way to pursue non-stereotypical personal interests or as diabolical conspirators who impose unwanted medical transition on "tomboyish" girls and young women. And it turns us into our own internalized

DOI: 10.4324/9781003053330-2

gatekeepers by persuading us that transition is legitimate only if we can justify it by discovering mysterious gendered essences within ourselves.

We are aware that our negativity about "gender identity" will take some readers by surprise, as this terminology has long been a staple of "trans 101" materials, and in the wider discourse it is strongly associated with the politics of trans rights, but we are not the first trans or allied authors to express doubts about this popular approach.[2] Many features of the standard narrative of transness – including its concept of "gender identity" – emerged from cis people's need for a way to think and talk about trans people that was not too *difficult* for the established order: one that did not really challenge its biases and preconceptions,[3] was not too inconvenient for its institutions and practices, did not threaten its established power structures, and did not require its "normal" inhabitants to face uncomfortable questions about themselves and their way of life.[4]

In this chapter, we will see many cases in which "gender identity" renders trans and gender-nonconforming people's needs, experiences, and sometimes our very existence unintelligible to others and occasionally even to ourselves. Our critique is not a claim that some particular group of people who use the term "gender identity" have invented it out of malice or intellectual laziness. Rather, the problem is social and systemic: "gender identity" is a shared resource for communicating about our gendered needs and our inner lives, but it's a shared resource that serves us badly.

There is a wealth of philosophical language for naming these types of social and systemic problems. In the jargon of social epistemologists like Fricker (2007) and Medina (2017), it enacts a *hermeneutical injustice:* that is, it gives us inadequate resources for understanding the experiences of an oppressed group (in this case trans people) because our resources developed under unjust conditions. To borrow another term from Nguyen (2021), it creates a *hostile epistemic environment*: that is, one that exploits people's vulnerability to error (in this case, by making false and harmful beliefs about trans people appear reasonable and natural).

2.1.1 *"Gender Identity" in the Received Narrative*

We'll start by sketching the received understanding of "gender identity" in the collective imagination:

1 People have a more-or-less stable inner trait called "gender identity".
2 One's "gender identity" is what disposes one to think of oneself as a "woman" or as a "man" (or, perhaps, as both or as neither).
3 One's "gender identity" is what disposes one to favor or avoid stereotypically feminine or masculine behaviors (or otherwise gendered behaviors).
4 It is possible for there to be a mismatch between one's "gender identity" and one's physiology (in particular one's "assigned sex" or "natal sex").
5 The frustration of these dispositions, or the presence of this sort of mismatch, results in a kind of distress known as "gender dysphoria" (or "gender incongruence").
6 The alleviation of "gender dysphoria" is the legitimate purpose of medical transition.
7 It is one's "gender identity", and not one's physiology, that properly determines whether one is a woman or a man (or both or neither).

Few people would endorse all of 1–7 without qualification, or would even regard them all as positions worth taking seriously, and trans theorists like Stone (1987), Spade (2003), and Bettcher (2014) have long criticized many components of this picture. Nevertheless, the prevailing discourse keeps returning to these assumptions, often with disastrous results. Relying on the language of "gender identity" (and the closely related concept of "gender dysphoria") to describe every aspect of trans subjectivity (and, indeed, of gendered subjectivity) contributes to concrete harms, including the three we sketch here.

2.1.2 Trans Unintelligibility and the Gatekeepers of Legitimacy

Historically, doctors have regulated trans people's access to medical treatment based on our ability to conform to gender stereotypes, withholding access to hormones and surgery unless their patients could demonstrate what they considered an acceptable level of femininity or masculinity (see Namaste, 2000, pp. 163–164; Spade, 2003; Gill-Peterson, 2018). This gatekeeping is linked to the received narrative, which is often endorsed by medical bodies that regulate trans care, and which can make pernicious forms of gatekeeping seem natural and appropriate.

Item 6 of the received narrative makes a diagnosis of "gender dysphoria" (or "gender identity disorder" or "gender incongruence") a crucial certificate of legitimacy for trans people seeking access to interventions like hormones or surgery. Setting aside general concerns about gatekeeping and medical paternalism, like those raised by Schulz (2018) and Tomson (2018), this makes a certain kind of sense if we understand "gender identity" in terms of 1 (it must be a stable inner trait), 4 (that can match or mismatch "natal sex"), and 5 (where this mismatch leads to "gender dysphoria").

But how can a prospective gatekeeper determine whether a trans patient truly has a "gender identity" incongruent with their assigned gender? Items 2 (which involves thinking of oneself as a "woman" or a "man") and 3 (which involves adopting stereotypically masculine or feminine behaviors) give them a whole suite of behavioral indicators of "gender identity". In particular, the appeal to masculinity and femininity in 3 implies that it is legitimate to consider the "evidence" of a patient's degree of (non) conformity to stereotypical norms of appearance and behavior for the "opposite" gender.

From a feminist perspective, this is absurd: why should the trappings of masculinity and femininity have anything to do with the legitimacy of one's desire to change one's physiology? Such indicators seem relevant only because the slew of claims we've listed are all presented as being about a single psychological phenomenon, known as "gender identity".

For all its absurdity, this kind of gatekeeping has until recently been enshrined in prevailing standards of trans care. The DSM-5 diagnostic criteria for Gender Dysphoria in adolescents and adults include, alongside feelings about one's "primary and/or secondary sex characteristics", "a strong desire to be treated as the other gender", and a "strong conviction that one has the typical feelings and reactions of the other gender (or some alternative gender different from one's assigned gender)" (American Psychiatric Association, 2013, pp. 452–453). In the previous version of the World Professional Association for Transgender Health's Standards of Care (SOC) (2012, pp. 20, 60, 106), access to some medical interventions was contingent on demonstrating one's masculinity or femininity through psychological evaluation or through experience "living in a gender role that is congruent with [one's] gender identity". (The current version explicitly rejects the earlier formulation; Coleman et al., 2022.)

The collective imagination of the medical establishment is gradually making room for the possibility that an individual might legitimately wish to change the configuration of their body without changing their pronouns or their wardrobe. But this change has been a long time in the making and will need our continued thought and vigilance to make sure that it sticks.

2.1.3 Trans Unintelligibility in Popular and Scholarly Discourse

The "gender identity" framework makes whole swaths of trans experience seem unintelligible in the wider culture. Scholars, pundits, readers, jurists, and politicians have trouble finding space for trans people in their imaginations, and the social and political consequences can be dire. The dominant conceptual resources provide thoughtless and hostile commentators with inspiration and talking points and leave the wider community ill-equipped to recognize their omissions and equivocations. The misrepresentations involved are numerous and varied, but we'll focus on two types.

In the first type of misrepresentation, cis commentators assume that trans people seek out medical transition out of a desire to conform to gender stereotypes. After all, "gender identity" is supposedly both an inclination toward stereotypically feminine or masculine behaviors (item 3 of the received narrative) and the thing that motivates and justifies medical transition (items 4–6). So trans people's investment in medical transition, these commenters claim, must stem from a misguided and fundamentally sexist impression that a certain sort of personality "goes with" certain sex characteristics.

A simple, crude instance of this problem can be seen in a long-time header image from the "gender critical" subreddit.

> (The image shows two figures, one a stylised male with a "feminine" pink circle over their head, one a stylised female with a "masculine" blue circle over their head, to represent a person who is AMAB (assigned male at birth, what would often be called "born biologically male") but has "feminine" interests, personality, or whatever, and a person who is AFAB (assigned female at birth, or "born biologically female") but has "masculine" style, or temperament, or whatever.)
>
> The image suggests that sexist society and "trans identity politics" are mirror images of each other: one tells people that they "must" change their personality to match their sex, the other tells people that they "must" change their sex to match their personality. Gender-critical feminism alone tells both these people that they are fine as they are.
>
> *(Roelofs, 2019)*

PATRIARCHY: NO!
You must change your personality to
match your sex!

TRANS IDENTITY POLITICS: NO!
You must change your sex to
match your personality!

GENDER CRITICAL FEMINISM:
You are both fine just the way you are.

Who are the big meanies here?

FIGURE 2.1   Roelofs's image

While this image never explicitly uses the term "gender identity", it invokes the popular "gender identity" framing by assuming that one thing is *both* the justification that "trans identity
politics" cites for medical transition and a set of "personality"
traits that the patriarchy deems appropriate to women but not
men or to men but not women.

Alas, such reasoning is not confined to the depths of Reddit.
Philosopher Jennifer McKitrick (2007, p. 147), for example, understands medical transition as resting on a stereotype-driven assumption that gendered behaviors and desires must "match" anatomy:

> While transsexuals may seem to challenge gender norms, in
> a sense, they embrace them. The desire to change one's body

to match one's perceived gender identity reveals acceptance of the idea that sex and gender must coincide, that certain behaviors and desires are incompatible with certain physical characteristics.

McKitrick has since rejected many aspects of her earlier approach (cf. McKitrick, 2015), but such views persist in philosophy. Stock (2019), for example, cites the DSM-5's definition of gender dysphoria as evidence that trans people transition because we see our personalities as conforming to the stereotypes of our chosen genders,[5] ignoring the fact that behavioral evidence is not treated as sufficient for a gender dysphoria diagnosis but rather serves as an additional (problematic) diagnostic *hurdle* for people seeking transition. Authors like Stock notice the medical establishment's adoption of the problematic received narrative and treat them as evidence that trans people's reasons for medical transition are similarly problematic.

The second type of misrepresentation involves the relationship between "gender identity" and gender category membership. According to a folk theory espoused in many trans communities, whether someone is a woman, a man, or something else depends largely or entirely on their "gender identity" (item 7 of the received narrative). In the simplest formulation, one is a man if and only if one *identifies as* a man, which involves some combination of believing oneself to be a man (or being disposed to believe this), being disposed to have a certain kind of positive emotional response to the prospect of being perceived to be a man, declaring oneself to be a man, and so on.[6]

But item 3 of the received narrative, which associates "gender identity" with stereotypically masculine or feminine behaviors, invites a reading of 7 on which trans people want to attribute gender category membership based on stereotypes. The crude version of this misreading can be seen in transphobic slogans like "wearing a dress doesn't make you a woman". While these slogans are literally true, their use falsely suggests that some important constituency of trans people *believes* that wearing a dress makes you a woman – a misrepresentation that is encouraged by the ambiguity of "gender identity".

A slightly more genteel version of the same misrepresentation is articulated by Sarah Ditum (2018), writing in *the Economist*:

> Feminism offers the radical proposition that what you like, what you wear and who you are should not be dictated by your chromosomes, hormones or any other marker of biological sex. Trans ideology reverses that. Perhaps men do like beer and women can't read maps, runs the theory, but some individuals have simply been assigned to the wrong category.

It only makes sense to attribute this view to "trans ideology" if one thinks that "trans ideology" includes items 3 and 7 of the received narrative and understands both of them in terms of a single phenomenon of "gender identity".

Like many authors, Andrew Sullivan (2019) partakes of these two misrepresentations simultaneously. Sullivan worries about "gender non-conforming kids falling prey to adult suggestions" that they should transition. He claims that

> [G]irly boys and tomboys are being told that gender trumps sex, and if a boy is effeminate or bookish or freaked out by team sports, he may actually be a girl, and if a girl is rough and tumble, sporty, and plays with boys, she may actually be a boy.

This looks like a conflation of "gender identity" as a criterion for category membership (7) with "gender identity" as an inclination toward masculine or feminine behavior (3). But Sullivan is ultimately concerned about kids "being led into permanent physical damage or surgery" – which takes "gender identity" as a reason for medical transition (5 and 6). He concludes with a plea to "leave those kids alone", framing the situation in terms of outside indoctrination and pressure rather than as an issue of young people's autonomy, self-authorship, or freedom to access interpretive resources not found in the dominant cissexist framework.[7]

These kinds of arguments and concerns all trade on the received narrative's picture of "gender identity". We do not claim that they would simply *disappear* without the ability to equivocate on "gender identity", but at least their advocates would be forced to fill in the missing steps: to tell us why we should expect the desire for medical transition and the desire to engage in stereotypically masculine or feminine behavior to be related in the way that they imagine. Making the case for the proposed connections explicit would then open them up to explicit critique.

In our view, relying on "gender identity" as the source of trans legitimacy creates a rhetorical vulnerability for trans people and our allies. It enables transphobic authors to proceed as if, once they show that "gender identity" is conceptually incoherent, metaphysically unpalatable, or empirically unfounded, or politically problematic, trans people and transness will simply disappear in a poof of logic. Rebecca Reilly-Cooper (2016), Alex Byrne (2020), and Kathleen Stock (2021) all go to great lengths to call attention to the problems and contradictions of the received concept of "gender identity" as they understand it, with Stock going so far as to list the view that everyone has "an important inner state called a gender identity" first among the "axioms of modern trans activism" at which she takes aim.

We likewise take a dim view of the received narrative of "gender identity". But objections to "gender identity" constitute some kind of devastating blow to trans politics only to the extent that trans politics needs "gender identity". If we can provide alternatives that do the same foundational work without the same baggage, then we think we are better off without it. Section 2.2 is devoted largely to developing one such alternative approach. If we are right that alternatives are available, then "gender identity" talk creates unnecessary confusions and propaganda vulnerabilities, allowing these authors and others to represent conceptual concerns about "gender identity" as serious obstacles that must be overcome before anyone is asked to entertain the possibility of trans legitimacy.

2.1.4 Trans Unintelligibility as an Obstacle to Self-Discovery

Denial and self-doubt are recurring, though by no means universal, themes in trans experience. Natalie Reed (2012a) describes some of the invalidating stories that trans people tell ourselves:

> "It's probably just a kink, a sex thing" . . . "doesn't everybody, on some level, sort of want to be the opposite sex?", "I should just learn to live with being a feminine man", "I just need to man-up, be more masculine, that will make it go away" . . . "maybe I can just cross-dress on weekends? That will be good enough" . . . "just my depression", "just my lack of confidence", "just my hatred of my identity", "just".

Why are these doubts so common? The reasons are many: life is uncertain, and the default presumption is, as Reed puts it, that "unless you're proven to be trans, you're cis". But the "gender identity" framing is another important contributing factor. Some trans people do find it useful, but for many of us, the search for an inner essence is counterproductive.

We speak from personal experience. Both of the authors spent years asking how we could really *know* our own gender identities, before deciding to give up on that and just start *trying* new names, new hormones, new personal aesthetics, and so on in a piecemeal, experimental manner, and discovering that some of them just "felt right" or otherwise significantly improved our lives.

Similar stories are widely circulated in the trans community, showing the progression from "I wish I were trans" or "if only I were trans then I could transition" to "no wait I am trans" has become a cliché in trans internet culture. S.J.S. Hancox-Li (2018) provides a representative description of the earlier stages of this process:

> I knew I wanted to be a woman; that was the easy part. But I kept hearing that I wasn't trans unless *I already was* a woman, in my heart at least. So I spent years looking around inside myself, trying to find this thing called Gender Identity, hoping it said Female on it. The weird part is that I never could. I still can't, frankly. I am a woman and still I can't find a gender identity in my heart (emphasis in original).

Critically, Hancox-Li's inability to find a "gender identity" was not rooted in any lack of clarity about what she wanted. She describes concrete, actionable gender desires that were already recognizable during her futile search for her "gender identity":

> I hated being covered in coarse hair and being an asshole and arguing instead of listening and wearing the baggiest clothes I could to hide the body that I hated and falling asleep every night dreading the person I would wake up as tomorrow.

Trans people who know they want to transition, and would be made happier by transition, can be derailed for a futile search for some mysterious inner state. What if there were a better source of insight into the question of whether to transition – one that was easy to access and whose practical relevance was clearer?

2.1.5 But Don't We Need Gender Identity?

In the next section, we'll introduce our preferred framework, but before we do, we'd like to briefly address a lingering concern. Trans people and our allies make heavy use of the language of "gender identity" and "gender dysphoria", suggesting that it is doing some real work for us. Can we really get by without it?

On a personal level, "gender identity" and "gender dysphoria" are sometimes useful or even necessary tools for navigating a cis-centric world. In an ideal world, doctors and insurance companies would provide health care using an informed consent model; in the actual world, a gender dysphoria diagnosis might be the only way to persuade them to provide the drugs and procedures that vastly improve our lives. In an ideal world, religious conservatives would respect our freedom to live as we please; in the actual world, we may need to appease them by pointing to supposedly deep, innate characteristics.

Also, we recognize that the "gender identity" framing might be the best compromise available in a hostile environment, and we don't fault activists for strategically using this conceptual tool against opponents. Unilaterally abandoning this language is not always a politically feasible choice. But we think the world would be better if everyone moved away from "gender identity" talk and toward something more like the framework that we develop in the rest of this chapter. And we think our framework is valuable in cooperative settings, where we are able to attend to what is true and explanatory rather than merely what is strategically useful against a hostile opponent.

Finally, we wish to note that our main concern is not the words "gender identity" but to the totalizing and essentialist character of the associated view of gendered subjectivity. In any given use, the term "gender identity" may be reaching for (and may successfully pick out) some largely unproblematic target concept. There are many such concepts; the problem is that they are many and often conflated.

Philosophical accounts of concepts called "gender identity" include Dembroff and St. Croix's (2019) concept of agential identity, which consists of political affiliation with a gender category, and Jenkins's (2018) concept of norm-relevancy, which corresponds roughly to the account of category-feels that we develop later in this chapter. These accounts pick out phenomena that are worth investigating, and it's possible that the words "gender identity" could be usefully repurposed to refer unambiguously to one of them.[8]

2.2 Gendered Traits and Gender Feels

We've pointed out some costs of the "gender identity" framing – but what's the alternative? In this section, we propose framing things in terms of gender *feels*: attitudes about one's relationships to various nonsubjective aspects of our shared material and social reality, which we'll refer to collectively as *gendered traits*.[9] By drawing distinctions among gendered traits, we can also distinguish different kinds of gender feels, which will help us see that no one thing satisfies all of items 1–7 of the received view. Instead, different kinds of gender feels are relevant to determining the appropriateness of medical transition, explaining why some people are drawn to particular gendered behaviors, and determining how someone prefers to be categorized. These distinctions are better placed than the "gender identity" framework to head off the confusions we discussed in Section 2.1.

2.2.1 Gendered Traits

Before we get to gender feels in Section 2.2.2, we'll give a taxonomy of gendered traits. These traits (like having a Y chromosome, wearing dresses, or being a man) are properties of people and are not primarily subjective psychological states; someone's having or lacking a particular gendered trait is part of shared social or material reality. We won't have a lot to say about what *makes* a trait gendered, other than that it depends on social norms and expectations; a trait that counts as gendered in one society need not count as gendered in others. (For more about the contingency and variability of our taxonomy, see Section 2.2.1.4)

We'll divide traits into three buckets, which we'll call *sexed biology*, *gendered behavior*, and (belonging to) *gender categories*. These three buckets serve as the *basic components* of our map of the sex/gender system: once we've introduced them, we will characterize other parts of the system in terms of them. In this chapter, we will use them to subdivide the gender feels that are typically lumped under the heading "gender identity". In Chapter 3, we will see that the same system of basic components helps us to classify gender norms.

Note that these three buckets of traits are basic in the sense that they are our analytic starting point, not in the sense that we think our concepts of them are acquired before other gender concepts, not in the sense that they are culturally universal, and not in the sense that they carve nature at its joints.

2.2.1.1 Sexed Biology

Sexed biology consists of those biological traits which are regarded as sex characteristics or are otherwise gendered. In the authors' society, these include having (or lacking) certain external genitalia (such as a penis, a clitoris, labia, and so on) and internal reproductive structures (such as a uterus, ovaries, a prostate, and so on), having certain combinations of X and Y chromosomes, producing certain types of gametes (ova or sperm), and various aspects of one's distribution of body hair, fat, and muscle.

In adopting the term "sexed biology", we do not mean to endorse anything like the traditional "sex"/"gender" distinction.[10] We could as easily say "gendered" biology, but our choice of terminology is a concession to the familiarity of this language: when viewed through the lens of the standard "sex"/"gender" picture, sexed biology is a major component of "sex". Sexed biology (very roughly) captures the traditional notion of bio-logical *sex characteristics* but is not concerned with any putative *sexes* or *sex categories* and doesn't include labels like "(biologi-cally) female" or "(biologically) male".[11] There might be reasons for biologists to posit "sexes" for the purposes of scientifically explaining reproduction and evolution (see Griffiths, 2021 for a thoughtful discussion of "sexes" interpreted in this way), but we are concerned with "sex" categorization in its capacity as a social practice, and in that capacity we are inclined to regard it as a kind of gender categorization.

Sexed biology in our sense isn't limited to "natural" or "endogenous" traits. For example, in the authors' society, it includes the trait of having a blood testosterone level below 5 nmol/L, whether or not that level is achieved with antiandrogen medications. This means that sexed biology includes some unexpected traits: since ear piercing is gendered in many societies, having pierced ears is an instance of sexed biology (in those societies).

2.2.1.2 Gendered Behavior

"Gendered behavior" is our cover term for those sorts of conduct to which a sex/gender system assigns gendered meaning. Here, we are appropriating "behavior" as a quasi-technical term, intended to include not just "behaviors" in the narrow intuitive sense but also less-active sorts of involvement in gendered practices or activities (so once someone has put on eye shadow, we'll say that they're displaying the behavior of wearing eye shadow, even though no further effort is required to keep the eye shadow on). We will also allow ourselves to be a bit sloppy in using the names of materials that play a key role in a behavior as shorthand for that behavior (so, for example, we might speak of "eye shadow" as a gendered behavior, when we mean the behavior of "wearing eye shadow").

Here are a few examples of gendered behaviors:

Gendered attire, which in the authors' culture includes skirts, neckties, and swimwear that does or doesn't cover one's nipples.

Grooming practices, such as using scented hygiene products, wearing or eschewing nail polish, and regular shaving or removal of underarm hair. This includes certain cases of passive involvement in such practices, such as receiving a gendered haircut, possibly against one's will.

Forms of labor and economic participation, such as child care, day-to-day home cleaning and food preparation, being a household's main "breadwinner", lifting heavy objects, and engaging in certain sorts of socially accepted or encouraged violence.

Interests, hobbies, and diversions, including games, sports, recreational craft activities, and film genres.

Communication style, expression of one's sexuality, and related behaviors, such as being relatively assertive or demure, or being more open or reserved in the expression of one's sexual experiences and desires.

This list is representative, not exhaustive.

2.2.1.3 Gender Categories

Gender categories are a type of social label or grouping to which individual people can belong (so that, for instance, we can say that Charles is a man or that Charlie is a woman).[12] Technically, *belonging to a gender category* (e.g., *being a man* or *being a woman*) is a trait, but as with "gendered behavior", we'll allow ourselves a bit of sloppy shorthand.

Woman/girl and *man/boy* are generally agreed to be gender categories. Other gender categories are recognized in certain trans and queer communities (e.g., *genderfluid*, *enby*, *demiguy*, and *agender*). Certain culture-specific labels (plausibly including *hijra*,[13] *burrnesha*,[14] *fa'afafine*, and *fa'atama*[15]), and medicalized gender-laden labels (e.g., *intersex*[16] or *endosex*[17]) might also be gender categories, although each raises its own complexities.[18] In this book, our attention will center on categories that are purely or primarily about gender classification, with little or no other descriptive content (so *father* and *actress* will not count as gender categories in our sense).

We won't assume that gender categories are mutually exclusive or exhaustive; we think it's possible to belong to multiple gender categories or perhaps none at all. Nor will we assume that any combination of biology and behavior suffices to determine or explain category membership. (In fact, we'll argue in Section 2.2.4 that gender category membership is not cognitively equivalent to any combination of biology and behavior, and in Chapter 5 that it is not metaphysically equivalent to any combination of biology and behavior.)

2.2.1.4 Contingent, Coarse-Grained, and Fuzzy?

We've divided gendered traits into three buckets – the three basic components of our map of the gender system. Readers might wonder: why those buckets? Why exactly three? How do we adjudicate which of them (if any) a trait belongs to?

Our three basic components are an expedient for understanding the workings of (and discourse around) certain social systems, not a representation of the True Nature of Things. There may be whole societies for which our taxonomy is not a good fit. There may in fact be whole societies for which the concept of a *gendered phenomenon* is not a good fit at all. In our society, some traits have gendered significance, and people largely agree about which traits those are. But we are not offering a theory of what it is to have gendered significance; for all we're claiming, the traits in our three buckets might have nothing in common beyond the fact that people group them together under the header "gender".

Given that we're in the business of sorting gendered traits into buckets, there is nothing magical about the number three. Other choices of basic components might be useful for other theoretical and practical projects; for instance, we could separate behavior into activities and artifacts; subdivide sexed biology into hormones, chromosomes, gametes, organs, and so forth; or combine gendered behavior and sexed biology under the general heading of material traits. Readers are invited to treat our taxonomy as a proof-of-principle whose details can be revised.

Once we've settled on a system of buckets, figuring out which trait to place in which bucket introduces additional fuzziness and arbitrariness. Whether a trait is gendered enough to belong in any of the buckets is culture-specific: covering one's hair might count as a gendered behavior in some societies, but a different kind of behavior in others. Similarly, hormones like estradiol and testosterone are gendered (and so part of sexed biology) in our society but would not count as sexed biology in a society that did not imbue them with gendered significance.[19] And within a given culture, we'll need to make some judgment calls about what counts as a gender category, an aspect of biology, or a gendered behavior. *Woman* and *man* are gender categories, but which other groupings count? What does it take for a sport or hobby to qualify as gendered? Which kinds of body modifications count as changes to sexed biology: bodybuilding, shaving, piercing, . . . all of the above?

In these cases, we should not expect – and do not need – a unique correct answer. Within our own culture, there are plenty of reasonably clear and intuitive cases of things that fall into specific buckets (like hormone levels for sexed biology, *woman* and *man* for gender categories, and wearing neckties for gendered behavior), and we're happy to admit that for some borderline cases there might simply be no fact of the matter.[20]

It often doesn't matter exactly where we place the boundaries: any *reasonable* way of drawing the borders will serve our purposes and allow for fruitful philosophical analysis. Just as the content of the buckets will vary with the society under study, so the proper approach to their delimitation may vary with the explanatory project: our framework is flexible and easily modified by design.

2.2.2 Gender Feels

Having introduced our three buckets of gendered traits, let's turn to the sorts of dispositions, attitudes, preferences, and emotions that are said to be facets or manifestations of one's inner "gender identity". These include, for example, a belief that one is a man or a woman or both or neither, a sense of wanting to wear dresses or of feeling *wrong* in a dress, a desire to grow breasts or an intense discomfort with one's breasts, eagerness or dread at the prospect of one's first beard growth, a disposition to be happier at some blood testosterone levels than one is at others, and so on. We're suspicious of "gender identity" talk, but these mental phenomena, which we'll call *gender feels*, are real and important.

We hope that our various examples give a reasonable sense of what sorts of things count as gender feels, but, for those interested in a bit more precision, *a gender feel about a gendered trait is an attitude or disposition about the fact or possibility of one's possessing that trait*. Let's unpack this a bit.

First, gender feels can be *attitudes or dispositions*. We are using the word "attitude" in (roughly) the broad sense common in analytic philosophy, so that it encompasses not just emotionally laden states like desiring an attribute or disliking an activity but also emotionally neutral states like believing a proposition or knowing a fact. One might not be fully conscious of all of one's attitudes or dispositions, and gender feels are meant to include attitudes and dispositions independent of whether one is explicitly conscious of them, oblivious to them, or in active denial about them. We take a broad view of what sorts of dispositions should be included here. For example, some people report that exogenous estradiol or testosterones make them feel more (or less) at home with the way they feel in their bodies or affect their emotional state in any of a number of other ways. This suggests that some of us are disposed to feel more comfortable at some hormone levels than others. We count such dispositions as gender feels, even if they are never manifested, since they are about estradiol and testosterone levels, which are part of sexed biology in our society.

Second, a gender feel is a disposition or attitude *about a certain fact or possibility*. Here we have in mind the broadest philosophical sense of the word "possibility" – something like *logical possibility* – including all sorts of hypothetical circumstances, past, present, and future, including those that are physically or metaphysically impossible or that have been foreclosed by the passage of time. Wishing that one had had stereotypically male physiology ten years ago (when one in fact did not) is a gender feel, even if time travel is impossible.

Third, this fact or possibility is a fact or possibility *about some gendered trait*. For present purposes, traits need not be stable properties or states: we include predicates like *operating power tools* or *being in the process of dyeing one's hair blue*. Examples of gender feels thus include *feeling dysphoric toward one's facial hair*, or *believing that one is a man*, or *having a deep sense of one's connection to a legacy of women in computer science*. While gendered traits are parts of a shared social and material world, gender feels are personal, experiential takes on them.

Fourth, a gender feel is about the fact or possibility *of one's possessing a trait*. That is, gender feels are the kinds of self-directed attitudes that philosophers refer to as *first-personal*.[21] An abstract philosophical belief in the equality of women and men, while laudable, does not count as a gender feel, because it makes no essential reference to the fact or possibility of oneself possessing a particular gendered trait.[22] Likewise, a feeling of disgust about men in skirts, or an equal-opportunity aesthetic objection to neckties on others, would not be a gender feel. (Of course, any of the aforementioned attitudes might be *caused by* some more personal gender feels in a particular instance.)

Because gender feels are about gendered traits, the classification of traits into buckets suggests a corresponding classification of feels. This gives us a distinction between biology-feels (such as the desire to grow breasts), category-feels (such as believing oneself to be a woman), and behavior-feels (such as an aversion to wearing lipstick). As Reed (2012b) notes, feels about one gendered trait need not entail "corresponding" feels about another: thinking of oneself as a man need not entail dysphoria about one's breasts or an aversion to stereotypically feminine clothing, and dysphoria about one's breasts need not entail dysphoria about one's genitals or (lack of) facial hair.

Gender feels have some important similarities to "gender identity". When people talk about an experience or manifestation of "gender identity", gender feel(s) are usually involved. But the concept of "gender feels" has less metaphysical baggage. It is customary to speak of someone having *a* gender identity, but most of us have *many* gender feels, which need not pattern together in any particular way. If we implicate "gender identity" in our discussion of how someone likes to wear button-up shirts, wishes they had a flat chest, and is more comfortable being called "he" and "sir", we are (or may be taken to be) suggesting that they have some single property that accounts for all these things. If we say these are some of their *gender feels*, we haven't made any commitment about whether there is a unified phenomenon at work. For many of us, there are richer causal connections among our gender feels, but the hypothesis that there is some single inner trait at work ought to be recognized *as a hypothesis*, not smuggled in as a presupposition. The possibility of such a unified "gender identity" may merit psychological study, but the question has no obvious bearing on the legitimacy (or illegitimacy) of trans people's self-reported category-feels, biology-feels, or behavior-feels.

2.2.3 But Isn't It Trivializing to Call Them "Feels"?

"Gender identity" sounds objective and serious; "gender feels" sound subjective and trivial. Isn't this a problem for advocates of trans rights?

We think the right response is to acknowledge that feels are subjective but deny that they are trivial. Our inner lives – including emotions and desires concerning things around us – are important. They deserve recognition and respect. In Chapter 4, we'll spend more time motivating and defending the thesis that trans people's gender feels deserve to be taken seriously, but for now, we want to flag that by embracing the word "feels", we mean to signal that inner experiences of gender are individual and perspectival and to refuse any presumption that this makes them unimportant or valueless.

2.2.4 Digression on Categories and Category-Feels

In our experience, gender categories and category-feels are the parts of our account that inspire the most suspicion. Testosterone and lip gloss (aspects of biology and behavior, respectively) may seem relatively concrete and straightforward, but it's a little harder to see what gender categories like *woman* and *man* add to the picture. Both folk theory and feminist scholarship often assume that gender categories can and should be explained away in terms of biology, behavior, and various psychosocial circumstances surrounding them. We will distinguish categories from all of these. Whether or not gender categories are metaphysically distinct from biology, behavior, etc., they are conceptually distinct.

As a matter of psychosocial reality, category-feels cannot be reduced to biology-feels or behavior-feels, and many queer communities have norms that treat category membership as distinct from either biology or behavior. We can illustrate both of these points using a stylized example, loosely based on the realities of the authors' lives and communities, in which three characters are (almost exactly) alike in their gendered behavior, sexed biology, behavior-feels and biology-feels but markedly different in their category-feels. We'll call them Ada, Blaise, and Cass.

Ada, Blaise, and Cass are indistinguishable in their sexed biology: all three have a 46,XX karyotype, and genitals, gonads, hormone levels, and so on that are unremarkable for individuals of this karyotype. (If it helps, the reader is welcome to imagine they are identical triplets.) They are also indistinguishable in their biology-feels. None of them have any interest in trying to remove or conceal any of their body or facial hair. All three

wear their scalp hair in the same crew cut, would like to be a
little more muscular than they are (and engage in similar weight
training programs in pursuit of this), and vaguely think that
they might want a breast reduction but haven't gotten around to
looking into it. All three use the same hormonal contraceptives
but are otherwise uninterested in taking exogenous hormones.

They are also indistinguishable with respect to gendered
behaviors, behavior-feels, and associated experiences. All three
shop mostly, but not exclusively, in the "men's" section and have
the same taste in flannel shirts. All three describe themselves as
pansexual and have similar taste in sexual and romantic partners.
All three were raised as girls and experienced adolescences made
predictably unpleasant by a society that considered them girls
and did its best to impose compulsory femininity on them.

All three have similar beliefs about the world at large and
similar personal and political values. They all consider themselves feminists, all hold their noses and vote for the same lesser
evil in each general election.

The key difference between Ada, Blaise, and Cass is their category-feels. Ada insists that she is a woman and bristles when called
"sir" or "him". Blaise insists that he is a man and bristles when
called "ma'am" or "her". Cass insists that they are nonbinary. Perhaps, when pressed with "But which are you *really*?", they answer
that they're "a cactus'" with a laugh that hides more than a little
frustration. They bristle about equally at "sir" and "ma'am" and
are about equally uncomfortable with "she" and "he" pronouns.[23]

Our three characters thus have very different category-feels,
in spite of their indistinguishable biology-feels and behavior-
feels. We could try to accommodate the difference by saying
they are distinguished by their behavior-feels, since being called
by gender terms like "man", gendered pronouns like "she" is a
behavior in our extended sense. But even if this works at a formal level, it is missing the point.

Our feels about particular words or grammatical features
are largely explained by our category-feels, together with

conventions that connect those linguistic phenomena with gender categories. Blaise doesn't just have feels about some finite
list of English words like "woman", "man", "she", and "he" –
he can be expected to develop corresponding feels about other
gendered words that English borrows or coins, and if he learns
another language, his feels about the grammar and vocabulary of
that language will most likely track with his prior category-feels.
This isn't to say that our feels about language can't come apart
from our category-feels in important ways, but only that trying to make this all about behavior-feels is missing an important
explanatory generalization. Besides, even if the reader would
prefer to do away with talk of gender categories and category-
feels in favor of gendered behavior and behavior-feels regarding
gendered language, similar questions will still arise about why
behavior-feels about gendered language are not determined by
other behavior-feels and biology-feels.

So Ada, Blaise, and Cass have different category-feels that
can't be fully explained by their behavior-feels and biology-feels.
According to the accepted norms of many trans-inclusive communities, they also belong to different gender categories based
on their category-feels: Ada is a cis woman, Blaise is a trans man,
and Cass is nonbinary. For all we've said so far, these norms
might be mistaken; *facts* about category membership might be
fully determined by other parts of the gender system. (We'll
argue in Chapter 5 that they are not mistaken and that it is right
to sort Ada, Blaise, and Cass into different categories.)

Whether or not these norms are mistaken, it's important to
be able to state them in a way that makes sense. And to do that,
we need to treat gender categories as at least cognitively distinct
from sexed biology, gendered behavior, and the associated feels
and experiences. Positing a separate bucket for gender categories,
alongside the buckets for sexed biology and gendered behavior,
is a helpful way to draw the requisite cognitive distinctions. (In
enriching our theoretical toolkit to separate conceptually distinct
entities, we follow a time-honored philosophical technique: just

consider all the senses, possible worlds, impossible worlds, situations, propositions, etc. that have been introduced to manage conceptual distinctions among things that might be connected by metaphysical necessity.)

Although Ada, Blaise, and Cass are fictional, they are not just outlandish characters cooked up for a contrived thought experiment. We can attest from personal experience that the sorts of traits, feels, and combinations thereof seen in these characters can be found in real people in many queer and trans communities and in our own social circles. This is not a matter of idle philosophical speculation: for many of us, it is a fact of everyday life.[24]

2.3 How Does This Help?

Having distinguished among different kinds of feels, we can now see that "gender identity" is used inconsistently in popular discourse: it refers sometimes to behavior-feels,[25] sometimes to category-feels,[26] and sometimes to biology-feels.[27] All three kinds of feels are worth talking about, but "gender identity" discourse encourages us to run them together. In cases where we would previously have talked about "gender identity", switching to "gender feels" forces us to ask ourselves what we are really trying to describe and what we really care about. Distinguishing among kinds of feels helps us to avoid the three problems with the received narrative from the beginning of this chapter.

2.3.1 Gatekeeping

The prevailing medical approach makes the ability to change one's sexed biology contingent on demonstrating one's "gender identity" by reporting certain category-feels and displaying gendered behaviors and attesting to behavior-feels deemed appropriate to one's gender category. Once we have the vocabulary to state this aspect of the prevailing approach explicitly, it becomes clear that its advocates owe us an explanation of why behavior-feels or category-feels should have any bearing on the appropriateness of interventions on sexed biology. Their relevance is not obvious, and it's particularly hard to see why stereotypically feminine or masculine behavior-feels should matter to someone who rejects sexist stereotypes. In contrast, it's easy to see why biology-feels are relevant: if a person would be happier and healthier with a different balance of hormones or genital configuration, this has clear implications for the pros and cons of the corresponding intervention on their sexed biology.

2.3.2 Popular and Academic Discourse

Distinguishing among gender feels also helps us correct the two misapprehensions from Section 2.1. The first misapprehension, that medical transition is motivated by a desire to conform to gender stereotypes, conflates biology-feels with behavior-feels. Once we distinguish them, it becomes obvious that biology-feels are the natural, default explanation for a desire to change one's sexed biology through medical transition, and that while a given person might have behavior-feels connected to their medical transition, those behavior-feels bear no special logical or metaphysical connection to the reasons for medical transition.

The second misapprehension, that trans politics must understand category membership in terms of (non-)conformity to gender stereotypes, looks much less plausible once we distinguish category-feels from behavior-feels. In trans-friendly spaces, category-feels are typically taken to settle questions about category membership (see our discussion of consensual gendering in Chapter 5), but gendered behaviors and behavior feels are not taken to entail much of anything about category membership or category-feels.

2.3.3 Self-Understanding

We've seen that trying to introspect a "gender identity" is a source of needless confusion and suffering for many trans people. In contrast, gender feels are often only modestly difficult to introspect (on a par with desires, tastes, and the like), and a given gender feel is often straightforwardly actionable. Someone who discovers that "ma'am", "she", "woman", and "sister" grate in a way that "sir", "he", "man", and "brother" do not, thereby knows something about their category-feels and has a good reason to ask their friends and colleagues to talk about them with the latter sort of language and not the former.[28] The same applies to behavior-feels (e.g., preferring the styling of women's blazers to men's blazers) and biology-feels (e.g., desire to grow breasts).

When introspection does fail, many kinds of feels suggest straightforward plans of experimental diagnosis. One way to start to figure out if one would feel better with a more estrogen-dominant hormonal balance is to go on hormone replacement for a couple of weeks or a couple of months and see how one feels about that. One way to figure out if one would prefer a more masculine name is to "try it on" for a bit in certain social spaces. One way to figure out if the person in the mirror would look less like a stranger with a different body shape is to try on a chest binder and take a look in the mirror.

The "gender identity" framing encourages us to get lost in distracting and irrelevant questions: it says that being trans is the proper reason to change your pronouns or your body, and that to be trans one must have a certain sort of "gender identity". This suggests that it's necessary to resolve a thorny, metaphysically loaded "who are you?" question before engaging with more straightforward and relevant "what do you want?" questions. And it demands the same answer to all the "what do you want?" questions at once, even though there's no obvious reason why anyone should need to figure out their relationship with pronouns in order to know whether they want to switch up their hormonal balance. As such, "gender identity" can be a significant unnecessary impediment to the process of trans self-discovery.[29]

The value of shifting attention from a search for "gender identity" to an examination of something more like feels has been noted by other trans writers. Twitter user MarleyMedusa writes:

> If you're wondering if you're trans, remember:
> The question "who am I really?" is a bottomless mystery of life. You can go around in circles F O R E V E R.
> Ask "How do I want to move in the world?" instead – all you have to do is try things until something helps.[30]

MarleyMedusa calls this "the first advice that ever helped me".[31]
Samantha Hancox-Li (2018) offers similar advice:

> Do you want to change your embodiment? Presentation? Pronouns? Go ahead and do it! You don't need some metaphysical voucher. You don't need an astronomer of the soul to detect the woman (or man) inside you. Become what you want and have fun with it!

The received conceptual apparatus of a unified "gender identity" makes it harder to discover and engage with the very aspects of the self that it strives to capture (as it did for Hancox-Li, for MarleyMedusa, and for us). That is a mark against it. We've aimed to develop a piecewise approach that is more conducive to a successful process of self-discovery and self-authorship, by treating distinct gender feels as independent and by classifying them into clusters on a project-specific basis.[32]

2.4 Precedents and Related Accounts

We are not the first to recognize the problems and conflations brought on by "gender identity" talk or to propose a finer-grained conceptual scheme for addressing them. Both Engdahl (2014) and Reed (2013) criticize standard framings of "gender identity" as essentialist and overly focused on cisgender perspectives.

Many trans and gender-nonconforming people have a base-line level of implicit or explicit awareness that different kinds of gender feels can come apart from each other,[33] and this aware-ness has given rise to a number of conceptual schemes that (in our terms) draw distinctions among different types of gender feels.

A common response to the medical gatekeeping and TERF rhetoric surrounding "gender identity" is to carve off "gender expression" (outwardly observable behaviors with gendered cultural significance or preferences and dispositions to engage in those behaviors) from "gender identity" (now understood as an inner state that justifies both claims on category member-ship and medical transition). This move helps by distinguishing the behavior-feels implicated in "gender expression" from the biology-feels that motivate medical transition and the category-feels that motivate claims of category membership. But it still conflates biology-feels and category-feels with each other. Moreover, usage in activist communities is inconsistent, and "gender identity" is often invoked when discussing a need or desire to engage in certain behaviors.[34]

The difficulty, as we see it, is that "gender identity" is being asked to do two rhetorical and expository jobs in conversations about trans rights and trans experience. First, we want it to be something internal and potentially important, so that the free-dom to realize it and act on it (including acting on it by engag-ing in gendered behaviors, by claiming category membership, or by modifying one's biology) is a legitimate moral and political priority. To do this work, "gender identity" needs to overlap with (or have implications for) behavior-feels. Second, "gender identity" needs to be *independent of* behavior-feels, so that it can do the work of explaining why our claims on category mem-bership and our desire for various interventions on our biology are inspired by something other than behavior-feels, and so are not just a misguided exercise in stereotype conformity. Our approach draws both of the needed distinctions without forcing them to compete for the same vocabulary. The distinction between gender feels and the various traits belonging to our three basic components allows the feels collectively to do the first job, and the separation of behavior from the other basic components, and the corresponding separation of behavior-feels from other feels does the second job.

Some authors posit versions of what we call biology-feels, alongside "gender expression" and "gender identity". Williams (2013) posits "gender orientation", which she glosses as "one's subjective experience of one's body, including its sexed attributes", and Finch (2016) posits "a sex relationship, meaning your feelings about your sex characteristics". The addition of a category for biology-feels is helpful – Williams uses it to critique conversion therapy – and represents the kind of insight that our approach seeks to systematize and generalize.

Serano's (2007, p. 77) concept of "subconscious sex" as a replacement for "gender identity" does some of the work of our biology-feels, though it also encompasses category-feels, and draws distinctions that are orthogonal to the ones that interest us (e.g., between subconscious and conscious mental states). Serano helpfully distinguishes subconscious sex from "intrinsic inclinations" toward masculine or feminine behaviors, which can be understood as a type of behavior-feels.

Finally, Reed (2012b) distinguishes gender feels more finely than we do, noting that feelings of dysphoria about different aspects of sexed biology (body hair, breasts, genitals, hormones, etc.) can occur independently of each other, and independently from feelings of dysphoria about cultural factors like names, pronouns, and attire. Reed's perspective calls attention to the limitations of any attempt to bundle gender feels into types, including ours: just as we should not expect biology-feels to have any consistent relationship with category-feels, so we should not expect all biology-feels to pattern with each other.

How should we understand the relationship between our proposal and these alternative ways of dividing things up? We think it would be a mistake to get too attached to precise taxonomic questions such as "how many kinds of feels are there?" or "is the desire to shave one's legs a behavior-feel or a biology-feel?" As we noted in Section 2.2.1.4, our division of the gender system into basic components was culturally contingent, coarse-grained, and fuzzy. Since we've classified gender feels in terms of the basic components at which they're directed, our taxonomy of gender feels inherits this contingency, coarse-grainedness, and fuzziness.[35]

Taking our list of basic components (or any proposed list of such components) too seriously, or uncritically accepting that they carve reality at the joints for all purposes, is dangerous. A given division of basic components may be useful for talking about some socially salient equivocations and hermeneutical injustices but not others. Any restructuring of the system of basic components (e.g., subdividing one or more of them to produce a system with more than three basic components) would suggest a corresponding restructuring of our classification of feels. The overall framework developed in this chapter and the next can be applied to any choice of basic components, so we hope (we think reasonably) that our general approach may remain useful even in situations where a different choice of basic components is required. This means that some of the alternative approaches from this section can be folded into the big-picture version of our approach, whose main point we can sum up as follows.

Talk of "gender identity" conflates distinct gender feels that come apart from each other in practice. We can understand these gender feels as self-situating attitudes toward gendered traits, which means that any way of classifying gendered traits induces a corresponding way of classifying gender feels. There's more of this approach to come – Chapter 3 will use the basic components of sexed biology, gendered behavior, and gender categories to classify gender norms.

Notes

1 Definitions include "a person's deeply felt, inherent sense of being a boy, a man, or male; a girl, a woman, or female; or an alternative gender (e.g., genderqueer, gender nonconforming, gender neutral)" (American Psychological Association, 2015), "[o]ne's innermost concept of self as male, female, a blend of both, or neither – how individuals perceive themselves and what they call themselves" (Human Rights Campaign, 2015), and "the all-encompassing feelings you have about which gender(s) you are or are not" (Reading, 2014).

2 See Section 2.4 in this chapter for a discussion of related approaches.

3 We have sometimes been permitted to be just interesting enough to serve as a "meal ticket" (in the words of Hale, 2009) for social and medical researchers, just shocking enough to meet the business needs of the sensationalist press, or just different enough to enable nice respectable liberals to pat themselves on the back for showing us minimal, half-hearted tolerance, but only as long as there was a way of "understanding" us that served these various consumers' appetites without forcing them to interrogate the foundations of their ways of thinking about gendered existence.

4 See Serano (2007), Namaste (2000), Prosser (1998), and Stone (1987) for various perspectives on the ways trans people adjust their self-presentation for the comfort of mainstream cis observers.

5 Or as she puts it, "developmentally, a personal narrative can emerge for some, over time, such that one takes what are perceived – by society and/or by oneself – to be feminine features of oneself as symptomatic of womanhood (or masculine features as symptomatic of manhood)."

6 Like most folk theories, this one is vague and underdeveloped in philosophically vexing ways, but its general spirit is clear enough in its subcultural context, and we are broadly sympathetic to it. In Chapter 5, we will formulate and defend a version of it that does not appeal to "gender identity" talk. What matters for the moment, though, is that there is a significant thread in trans politics which holds that being a woman involves "identifying as a woman", being a man involves "identifying as a man", and so on, where claims about "identifying as" are taken to be claims about one's "gender identity".

7 For more discussion of the importance of access to interpretive resources and of the type of rhetorical maneuver that Sullivan is

employing here, see George and Goguen (2021). For further discussion of trans youth issues, including some positive cases for youth transition and some replies to the kinds of concerns that raised in Sullivan (2019), see Ashley (2019a, 2019b, 2019c, 2020, 2021a, 2021b); Wenner & George (2021); George & Wenner (2019); Priest (2019); Burns (2019, 2020); Serano (2016, 2017, 2018, 2020); Jones (2016, 2017, 2020, 2021a, 2021b, 2021c); and the sources cited therein.

8 We do disagree with Jenkins's suggestion that the entity she picks out is best suited explaining and justifying trans people's need for medical transition; we think our biology-feels do a better job of that. But Jenkins's claim as stated is very weak; she says that her account of the entity she calls "gender identity" is "*compatible* with the idea that *some* trans people have a need for transition related health care that is based on their gender identity" (emphasis ours). As long as those qualifiers are in place, we basically agree.

9 That is, we are adopting "gendered trait" as a convenient umbrella term for the various stuff about which individuals have gender feels and about which societies have gender norms. This usage does not perfectly track either colloquial or philosophical use of the word "trait", but some umbrella term is needed, and we think this one represents a reasonable compromise.

10 According to the traditional "sex/gender" distinction, sexes (usually called "male" and "female") are natural biological categories while genders (usually called "man" and "woman") are social categories built atop them. See Mikkola (2019) for an overview.

11 We don't think that anything in this chapter requires one to completely reject such categories; what is important here is just that our notion of sexed biology doesn't depend on them. See Freeman & López (2018) for more on the possibility of taking sex characteristics seriously while rejecting sex categories.

12 This characterization of gender categories will serve us well enough here, but we will have reason to modify it in Chapter 5, where we work through some more technical details.

13 *Hijra* is a gender-associated label or category associated with the South Asian cultural context. See Sequeira (2022); Dutta (2013); Reddy (2010); and the sources cited therein for further discussion.

14 *Burrnesha* is a gender-associated label or category associated with the Albanian cultural context. See Robertson Martinez (2021) and Young & Eicher (2001) for further discussion.

15 *Fa'afafine*, and *fa'atama* are gender-associated labels or categories associated with the Samoan cultural context. See Lim-Bunnin (2020); McMullin (2011); Farran (2010); Schmidt (2001); and the sources cited therein for further discussion.

16 *Intersex* is an umbrella term for people whose sexual or reproductive anatomy doesn't match medical expectations of typical development. See InterACT (2021); Intersex Initiative (2008); and Holmes (2008) for further discussion.

17 *Endosex* is an antonym or approximate antonym for "intersex". It plays a role very roughly analogous to words like "cisgender", "heterosexual", "abled", "neurotypical", and so on in explicitly marking a dominant or "normal" group instead of simply allowing it to be treated as a default.

18 The question of when exactly a social label or grouping is a gender category in our sense (as opposed to some other kind of social feature) can be difficult: many specific cases will be politically fraught or will not admit clear answers. Characterizing specific labels as *competing* gender categories or as "third genders" or "none of the above" options can be worrisomely exoticizing or othering, and we are not qualified to speak for, say, the hijra community or the intersex community. (See, e.g., Lim-Bunnin, 2020; la Pavona, 2021a, 2021b; Carpenter, 2018; Dutta, 2013, 2014; Dutta & Roy, 2014; Hossain, 2018, and Chapter 7 of Serano, 2007 for a few perspectives on the diverse issues involved.) But we do wish to emphasize three features of our approach that we think limit (but do not eliminate) some concerns about extending the "gender category" framework to these cases. First, in our account, gender categories are not assumed to be disjoint, so being a member of one category doesn't make one's membership in another category impossible or "second rate". Second, our choice of the term "gender category" is not meant to endorse a sex/gender distinction: categories purporting to be "sexes" are gender categories as well, or, if they are not, they are to be ruled out on other grounds. Third, we can apply the general approach to almost any choice of a collection of gender categories, so if different decisions about what counts as a gender category turn out to be appropriate for different tasks, the rest of our framework is flexible enough to accommodate this. Our omission of some other social categories, such as *cisgender*, *transgender*, *femme*, *bottom*, *butch*, and *bear*, is not meant to rule out the possibility of including them as gender categories,

although they are not the main focus of this book's treatment of categories.

19 Of course, people in a society that does not imbue these hormones with gendered significance will still have these hormones, which may influence observable traits that do count as part of sexed biology in that society.

20 Some metaphysicians, including Graff Fara (Graff, 2000; Fara, 2008), Williamson (1994), and Sorensen (1988, 2001), hold that there is always a fact of the matter, and what looks like metaphysical indeterminacy is better explained using other philosophical tools. We're not trying to pick a fight with those metaphysicians. Whatever precise story you use to characterize the fuzzy boundaries between the tall and the non-tall, the deep difficulty of assessing counterfactuals like "if I had an older brother, he would like potato pancakes", the failure of a superposed quantum system to determine any particular state in the measurement basis, or the openness of the future . . . we're claiming that a similar phenomenon occurs at the edges of our buckets.

21 Some prominent theories of first-person attitudes are offered by Anscombe (1975), Perry (1979), Lewis (1979), and Bermúdez (1998).

22 Of course, we can describe a belief in the equality of men and women in first-person terms, as a desire to live in a world where men and women are equal or a belief that one lives in a world where men and women ought to be equal. But this reference to oneself is inessential to the attitude and doesn't capture what the attitude is really about.

23 The reader is free to invent any number of variations on this story, symmetrically adjusting the biology, appearance, associated feels, and sexual preferences of the three characters.

24 What might Ada, Blaise, and Cass think of each other? If they all embrace the norms of more inclusive queer communities, then they will take each other's gender category claims seriously. They might still wonder what chance events might have steered them toward different category-feels, but they need not find each other especially perplexing or threatening. This outcome strikes us as plausible: in our experience of queer communities, peaceful coexistence is not uncommon in these cases. For the most part, it's what we will assume about them going forward. That said, it is easy to imagine other kinds of scenarios. It's not hard to

imagine a version of this story in which Ada finds Blaise and Cass threatening, taking their claims of being non-somen as an attack on her status as a woman in good standing. Unfortunately, this version of the story has also come up in our own experiences. A major goal of this text – and of the project of separating out categories and category-feels in the manner that we've begun to do here – is to clarify that the former option is coherent, and that Ada, Blaise, and Cass do not need to find each other threatening in this way.

25 A few examples: in the Huffington Post, Tobia (2014) writes: "While people may try to discriminate against me and tell me that I'm dressing 'inappropriately' for work, I will hold on to my gender identity and sense of self"; The 2015 US Transgender Survey estimates that 27% of respondents who were out to their families were "not allowed to wear clothes matching their gender identity" (James et al., 2016, p. 70).

26 This understanding is common trans community discourse about how "gender identity" determines gender category membership, even for people who do not intend to medically transition (so that biology-feels are not implicated) or for feminine trans men, masculine trans women, and traditionally feminine or masculine nonbinary people (so that behavior-feels are not implicated).

27 This understanding underlies many discussions about "gender identity" as the motive for medical transition.

28 Do the category-feels *constitute* reasons for action, or are they merely *indicative* of reasons for action? Philosophers in the literature on reasons will disagree, but settling this dispute is not important to what we're doing here.

29 See Bettcher (2014) for a related critique of the "trapped in the wrong body" model of trans identity and a proposal that "woman" and "man" admit of multiple meanings. Our discussion of gender feels makes no direct appeal to the meanings of "woman" and "man", though see Chapter 5 for our views on the categories *woman* and *man*.

30 https://twitter.com/marleymedusa/status/1007740977128198144

31 https://twitter.com/marleymedusa/status/1009247171084836864

32 The piecewise approach also implicitly rejects the assumption that different gender feels or transition steps must inevitably come as a package. Insofar as anyone's transition involves confused, mistaken, or subsequently regretted steps informed by a "package deal"

assumption, our approach seems like a reasonable way to try to head that off. To the best of our knowledge, such cases are extremely rare, but the specter of such "package deal" reasoning (in particular, of reasoning that behavior-feels and biology-feels must pattern together) is a major "concern" of many pundits, so we want to highlight that, in making transition more conceptually accessible, our approach does not encourage this kind of confusion.

33 A letter-writer in a recent Autostraddle advice column (Osworth, 2019) asks, "How do you differentiate between gender-expression feels and gender-itself feels?".

34 Examples of such usage can be found in, for example, Tobia (2014) or Burns (2019).

35 Our notion of gender feels also admits another sort of refinement, as it lumps together phenomena that are heterogenous from a classic philosophy of mind perspective: beliefs, desires, expectations, dispositions and inclinations; proprioceptive experiences of one's body; and so on. Related heterogeneity concerns about "gender identity" are taken up by some other authors, including Bettcher's (2009), who distinguishes between metaphysical and existential self-identity, and Roman (2019), who distinguishes belief and desires about gendered traits. Our system could be refined to accommodate such distinctions, but we leave that refinement as a problem for another time or for other philosophers.

References

American Psychiatric Association. (2013). *Diagnostic and statistical manual of mental disorders* (5th ed.). APA. https://doi.org/10.1176/appi.books.9780890425596

American Psychological Association. (2015). Guidelines for psychological practice with transgender and gender nonconforming people. *American Psychologist, 70*(9), 832–864. https://doi.org/10.1037/a0039906

Anscombe, G. E. M. (1975). The first person. In *Mind & language: Wolfson college lectures 1974* (pp. 45–65). Clarendon Press.

Ashley, F. (2019a). Thinking an ethics of gender exploration: Against delaying transition for transgender and gender creative youth. *Clinical Child Psychology and Psychiatry, 24*(2), 223–236. https://doi.org/10.1177/1359104519836462

Ashley, F. (2019b). Shifts in assigned sex ratios at gender identity clinics likely reflect changes in referral patterns. *The Journal of Sexual Medicine, 16*(6), 948–949. https://doi.org/10.1016/j.jsxm.2019.03.407

Ashley, F. (2019c). Watchful waiting doesn't mean no puberty blockers, and moving beyond watchful waiting. *The American Journal of Bioethics, 19*(6), W3–W4. https://doi.org/10.1080/15265161.2019.1599466

Ashley, F. (2020). Homophobia, conversion therapy, and care models for trans youth: Defending the gender-affirmative approach. *Journal of LGBT Youth, 17*(4), 361–383. https://doi.org/10.1080/19361653.2019.1665610

Ashley, F. (2021a). Flawed reasoning on two dilemmas: A commentary on Baron and Dierckxsens. *Journal of Medical Ethics, 48*, 637–638. https://doi.org/10.1136/medethics-2021-107647

Ashley, F. (2021b). The clinical irrelevance of "desistance" research for transgender and gender creative youth. *Psychology of Sexual Orientation and Gender Diversity, 9*, 387–397. https://doi.org/10.1037/sgd0000504

Bermúdez, J. L. (1998). *The paradox of self-consciousness: Representation and mind.* MIT Press.

Bettcher, T. M. (2009). Trans identities and first-person authority. In L. Shrage (Ed.), *You've changed: Sex reassignment and personal identity* (pp. 98–120). Oxford University Press.

Bettcher, T. M. (2014). Trapped in the wrong theory: Rethinking trans oppression and resistance. *Signs: Journal of Women in Culture and Society, 39*(2), 383–406. https://doi.org/10.1086/673088

Burns, K. (2019, November 11). The battle over Luna younger, a 7-year-old trans girl in Texas, explained. *Vox.* www.vox.com/identities/2019/11/11/20955059/luna-younger-transgender-child-custody

Burns, K. (2020, December 30). No, lesbians aren't "going extinct." *Medium.* https://katelynburns.medium.com/no-lesbians-arent-going-extinct-20a7a3aef448

Byrne, A. (2020). Are women adult human females? *Philosophical Studies, 177*(12), 3783–3803. https://doi.org/10.1007/s11098-019-01408-8

Coleman, E., Radix, A. E., Bouman, W. P., Brown, G. R., de Vries, A. L. C., Deutsch, M. B., Ettner, R., Fraser, L., Goodman, M., Green, J., Hancock, A. B., Johnson, T. W., Karasic, D. H., Knudson, G. A., Leibowitz, S. F., Meyer-Bahlburg, H. F. L., Monstrey, S. J.,

Motmans, J., Nahata, L., . . . Arcelus, J. (2022). Standards of care for the health of transgender and gender diverse people, version 8. *International Journal of Transgender Health*, *23*(Supp. 1), S1–S259. https://doi.org/10.1080/26895269.2022.2100644

Dembroff, R., & St. Croix, C. (2019). 'Yep, I'm Gay': Understanding agential identity. *Ergo: An Open Access Journal of Philosophy*, *6*, 571–599.

Ditum, S. (2018, July 5). Trans rights should not come at the cost of women's fragile gains. *The Economist*. www.economist.com/open-future/2018/07/05/trans-rights-should-not-come-at-the-cost-of-womens-fragile-gains

Dutta, A. (2013). An epistemology of collusion: Hijras, Kothis and the historical (dis) continuity of gender/sexual identities in Eastern India. In *Gender history across epistemologies* (pp. 305–329). John Wiley & Sons, Ltd. https://doi.org/10.1002/9781118508206.ch14

Engdahl, U. (2014). Wrong body. *TSQ: Transgender Studies Quarterly*, *1*(1–2), 267–269. https://doi.org/10.1215/23289252-2400226

Fara, D. G. (2008). Profiling interest relativity. *Analysis*, *68*(4), 326–335. https://doi.org/10.1093/analys/68.4.326

Farran, S. (2010). Pacific perspectives: Fa'afafine and Fakaleiti in Samoa and Tonga: People between worlds. *Liverpool Law Review*, *31*(1), 13–28. https://doi.org/10.1007/s10991-010-9070-0

Finch, S. D. (2016, August 10). Transgender 101: A guide to gender and identity to help you keep up with the conversation. *Everyday Feminism*. https://everydayfeminism.com/2016/08/transgender-101/

Freeman, L., & López, S. A. (2018). Sex categorization in medical contexts: A cautionary tale. *Kennedy Institute of Ethics Journal*, *28*(3), 243–280. https://doi.org/10.1353/ken.2018.0017

Fricker, M. (2007). *Epistemic injustice: Power and the ethics of knowing*. Oxford University Press.

George, B. R. & Goguen, S. (2021) Hermeneutical backlash: trans youth panics as epistemic injustice. *Feminist Philosophy Quarterly* 7(4). https://ojs.lib.uwo.ca/index.php/fpq/article/view/13518

George, B. R., & Wenner, D. M. (2019). Puberty-blocking treatment and the rights of bad candidates. *The American Journal of Bioethics*, *19*(2), 80–82. https://doi.org/10.1080/15265161.2018.1557287

Gill-Peterson, J. (2018). *Histories of the transgender child*. University of Minnesota Press.

Graff, D. (2000). Shifting sands: An interest-relative theory of vagueness. *Philosophical Topics*, *28*(1), 45–81. https://doi.org/10.5840/philtopics20002816

Griffiths, P. E. (2021). *What are biological sexes?* 28.

Hale, J. (2009). *Suggested rules for non-transsexuals writing about transsexuals, transsexuality, transsexualism, or trans _____*. https://sandystone.com/hale.rules.html

Hancox-Li, S. (2018, December 21). The dark matter of the soul. *Sjshancoxli.* www.sjshancoxli.com/post/2018/12/21/the-dark-matter-of-the-soul

Holmes, M. (2008). *Intersex: A perilous difference.* Rosemont Publishing & Printing Corp.

Human Rights Campaign. (2015). Glossary of terms. *HRC.* www.hrc.org/resources/glossary-of-terms

InterACT: Advocates for Intersex Youth. (2021, February 19). Intersex definitions. *InterACT: Advocates for Intersex Youth.* https://interactadvocates.org/intersex-definitions/

Intersex Initiative. (2008). Intersex FAQ (frequently asked questions). *Intersex Initiative.* http://intersexinitiative.org/articles/intersex-faq.html

James, S. E., Herman, J. L., Rankin, S., Keisling, M., Mottet, L., & Anafi, M. (2016). *The report of the 2015 U.S. transgender survey.* The National Center for Transgender Equality. https://transequality.org/sites/default/files/docs/usts/USTS-Full-Report-Dec17.pdf

Jenkins, K. (2018). Toward an account of gender identity. *Ergo: An Open Access Journal of Philosophy*, *5*, 713–744. https://doi.org/10.3998/ergo.12405314.0005.027

Jones, Z. (2016, December 1). Debunking hypothetical arguments about youth transition. *Gender Analysis.* https://genderanalysis.net/2016/12/debunking-hypothetical-arguments-about-youth-transition-gender-analysis/

Jones, Z. (2017, November 30). Why the "youth transition as anti-gay conversion therapy" myth doesn't add up. *Gender Analysis.* https://genderanalysis.net/2017/11/why-the-youth-transition-as-anti-gay-conversion-therapy-myth-doesnt-add-up/

Jones, Z. (2020, December 31). Lesbocalypse now: Elliot page took nothing from you [Text]. *GenderAnalysis.* https://genderanalysis.net/2020/12/lesbocalypse-now-elliot-page-took-nothing-from-you/

Jones, Z. (2021a, April 30). What parents don't know: Trans youth study reveals fatal flaw at the heart of "rapid-onset gender dysphoria" (ROGD) pseudo-diagnosis (1 of 3). *Gender Analysis.* https://genderanalysis.net/2021/04/what-parents-dont-know-trans-youth-study-reveals-fatal-flaw-at-the-heart-of-rapid-onset-gender-dysphoria-rogd-pseudo-diagnosis-1-of-3/

Jones, Z. (2021b, May 1). What parents don't know: Trans youth study reveals fatal flaw at the heart of "rapid-onset gender dysphoria" (ROGD) pseudo-diagnosis (2 of 3). *Gender Analysis*. https://genderanalysis.net/2021/05/what-parents-dont-know-trans-youth-study-reveals-fatal-flaw-at-the-heart-of-rapid-onset-gender-dysphoria-rogd-pseudo-diagnosis-2-of-3/

Jones, Z. (2021c, May 1). What parents don't know: Trans youth study reveals fatal flaw at the heart of "rapid-onset gender dysphoria" (ROGD) pseudo-diagnosis (3 of 3). *Gender Analysis*. https://genderanalysis.net/2021/05/what-parents-dont-know-trans-youth-study-reveals-fatal-flaw-at-the-heart-of-rapid-onset-gender-dysphoria-rogd-pseudo-diagnosis-3-of-3/

la Pavona, K. (2021a, December 10). Thread beginning "I think about this image a lot . . ." [Tweet]. *Twitter*. https://twitter.com/binaryAegis/status/1469344337439834118

la Pavona, K. (2021b, December 17). Thread beginning "I want to revisit this thread . . ." [Tweet]. *Twitter*. https://twitter.com/binaryAegis/status/1471867940068896769

Lewis, D. (1979). Attitudes de Dicto and de Se. *Philosophical Review*, *88*(4), 513–543. https://doi.org/10.2307/2184843

Lim-Bunnin, L. L. (2020). "And every word a lie": Samoan gender-divergent communities, language and epistemic violence. *Women's Studies Journal*, *34*(1/2), 76–91.

McKitrick, J. (2007). Gender identity disorder. In *Establishing medical reality: Essays in the metaphysics and epistemology of biomedical science* (pp. 137–148). Springer.

McKitrick, J. (2015). A dispositional account of gender. *Philosophical Studies*, *172*(10), 2575–2589. https://doi.org/10.1007/s11098-014-0425-6

McMullin, D. T. (2011). Fa'afine notes: On Tagaloa, Jesus, and Nafuna. In Q.-L. Driskill, C. Finley, & B. J. Gilley (Eds.), *Queer indigenous studies: Critical interventions in theory, politics, and literature* (pp. 114–131). University of Arizona Press.

Medina, J. (2017). Varieties of hermeneutical injustice. In *The Routledge handbook of epistemic injustice* (pp. 41–52). Routledge.

Mikkola, M. (2019). Feminist perspectives on sex and gender. In *Stanford encyclopedia of philosophy*. https://plato.stanford.edu/entries/feminism-gender/

Namaste, V. (2000). *Invisible lives: The erasure of transsexual and transgendered people*. University of Chicago Press.

Nguyen, C. T. (2021). The seductions of clarity. *Royal Institute of Philosophy Supplements*, *89*, 227–255. https://doi.org/10.1017/S1358246121000035

Osworth, A. E. (2019, January 29). You need help: How do I tell If I'm a butch cis woman or a trans non-binary person? *Autostraddle*. www.autostraddle.com/you-need-help-how-do-i-tell-if-im-a-butch-cis-woman-or-a-trans-non-binary-person-440266/

Perry, J. (1979). The problem of the essential indexical. *Noûs*, *13*(1), 3–21. https://doi.org/10.2307/2214792

Priest, M. (2019). Transgender children and the right to transition: Medical ethics when parents mean well but cause harm. *The American Journal of Bioethics*, *19*(2), 45–59. https://doi.org/10.1080/1526 5161.2018.1557276

Prosser, J. (1998). *Second skins: The body narratives of transsexuality*.

Reading, W. (2014, May 15). Separating out gender identity from gender expression. *Everyday Feminism*. https://everydayfeminism.com/2014/05/separating-identity-expression/

Reddy, G. (2010). *With respect to sex: Negotiating hijra identity in South India*. University of Chicago Press.

Reed, N. (2012a, April 17). The null HypotheCis. *Sincerely, Natalie Reed*. https://freethoughtblogs.com/nataliereed/2012/04/17/the-null-hypothecis/

Reed, N. (2012b, May 1). Different dysphorias and esoteric embodiments. *Sincerely, Natalie Reed*. https://web.archive.org/web/20121124202952/http://freethoughtblogs.com/nataliereed/2012/05/01/different-dysphorias-and-esoteric-embodiments/

Reed, N. (2013, March 9). Born this way (reprise): The new essentialism. *Sincerely, Natalie Reed*. https://freethoughtblogs.com/nataliereed/2013/03/09/born-this-way-reprise-the-new-essentialism/

Reilly-Cooper, R. (2016, May 13). Why self-identification shouldn't be the only thing that defines our gender. *The Conversation*. http://theconversation.com/why-self-identification-shouldnt-be-the-only-thing-that-defines-our-gender-57924

Robertson Martinez, E. (2021). *Social representations and women who live as men in Northern Albania* [Thesis, University of Cambridge]. https://doi.org/10.17863/CAM.72219

Roelofs, L. (2019, July 25). Dear philosophers, you can trust the feminist consensus: Gender-critical radical feminism is bogus. *Majestic*

Equality. https://majesticequality.wordpress.com/2019/07/25/dear-philosophers-you-can-trust-the-feminist-consensus-gender-critical-radical-feminism-is-bogus/

Roman, A. (2019, September 11). *Gender desire vs. gender identity*. https://medium.com/@kemenatan/gender-desire-vs-gender-identity-a334cb4eeec5

Schmidt, J. (2001). Redefining Fa'afafine: Western discourses and the construction of transgenderism in Samoa. *Intersections, 6.* http://intersections.anu.edu.au/issue6/schmidt.html#n16

Schulz, S. L. (2018). The informed consent model of transgender care: An alternative to the diagnosis of gender dysphoria. *Journal of Humanistic Psychology, 58*(1), 72–92. https://doi.org/10.1177/0022167817745217

Sequeira, R. (2022). Show and tell: Life history and hijra activism in India. *Signs: Journal of Women in Culture and Society, 47*(2), 451–474. https://doi.org/10.1086/716645

Serano, J. (2007). *Whipping girl: A transsexual woman on sexism and the scapegoating of femininity*. Seal Press.

Serano, J. (2016). Detransition, desistance, and disinformation: A guide for understanding transgender children . . . *Medium*. https://juliaserano.medium.com/detransition-desistance-and-disinformation-a-guide-for-understanding-transgender-children-993b7342946e

Serano, J. (2017). Transgender agendas, social contagion, peer pressure, and prevalence. *Medium*. https://juliaserano.medium.com/transgender-agendas-social-contagion-peer-pressure-and-prevalence-c3694d11ed24

Serano, J. (2018). Everything you need to know about rapid onset gender dysphoria. *Medium*. https://juliaserano.medium.com/everything-you-need-to-know-about-rapid-onset-gender-dysphoria-1940b8afdeba

Serano, J. (2020). Transgender people, "gay conversion," and "lesbian extinction": What the data show. *Medium*. https://juliaserano.medium.com/transgender-people-gay-conversion-and-lesbian-extinction-what-the-data-show-dea2a3e70174

Sorensen, R. A. (1988). *Blindspots*. Oxford University Press.

Sorensen, R. A. (2001). *Vagueness and contradiction*. Oxford University Press.

Spade, D. (2003). Resisting medicine, re/modeling gender. *Berkeley Women's Law Journal, 18*, 15–37.

Stalnaker, R. (2002). Common ground. *Linguistics and Philosophy, 25*(5–6), 701–721. https://doi.org/10.1023/a:1020867916902

Stock, K. (2019). Response to Roelofs (part two) – Kathleen Stock – Medium. *Archive.Is.* http://archive.is/XwXU8

Stock, K. (2021). *Material girls: Why reality matters for feminism.* Fleet.

Stone, S. (1987). The empire strikes back: A posttranssexual manifesto. *Camera Obscura: Feminism, Culture, and Media Studies, 10*(2), 150–176. https://doi.org/10.1215/02705346-10-2_29-150

Sullivan, A. (2019, September 20). When the ideologues come for the kids. *Intelligencer.* https://nymag.com/intelligencer/2019/09/andrew-sullivan-when-the-ideologues-come-for-the-kids.html

Tobia, J. (2014, June 10). Why I'm genderqueer, professional and unafraid. *HuffPost.* www.huffpost.com/entry/genderqueer-professional-_b_5476239

Tomson, A. (2018). Gender-affirming care in the context of medical ethics – gatekeeping v. informed consent. *South African Journal of Bioethics and Law, 11*(1), Article 1. https://doi.org/10.7196/SAJBL.2018.v11i1.00616

Wenner, D. M., & George, B. R. (2021). Not just a tragic compromise: The positive case for adolescent access to puberty-blocking treatment. *Bioethics, 35*, 925–931. https://doi.org/10.1111/bioe.12929

Williams, C. (2013, January 16). Gender orientation, identity, and expression. *TransAdvocate.* www.transadvocate.com/gender-orientation_n_8267.htm

Williamson, T. (1994). *Vagueness.* Routledge.

Williamson, T. (1995). Definiteness and knowability. *Southern Journal of Philosophy, 33*(S1), 171–192. https://doi.org/10.1111/j.2041-6962.1995.tb00769.x

World Professional Association for Transgender Health. (2012). *Standards of care for the health of transsexual, transgender, and gender nonconforming people* (7th Version). www.wpath.org/publications/soc

Young, A., & Eicher, J. B. (2001). *Women who become men: Albanian sworn virgins* (1st ed.). Berg Publishers.

3

DON'T HATE THE PLAYER

Traits Versus Norms

3.1 Gender Norms

So far we've suggested replacing the notions of "gender" and "gender identity" with a more fine-grained conceptual scheme that posits gendered traits (which we divide into sexed biology, gender categories, and gendered behavior) and feels about those traits. These tools help us pull apart different senses of "gender" and criticize some harms of the gender system, like the medical gatekeeping we discussed in Chapter 2. But they don't let us distinguish all of the relevant senses of "gender" (what happened to the "oppressive system that ties certain behaviors and characteristics to sex" from Problematic Slogan 2 in Chapter 1?) or critique the most famous harms of the gender system.

Many of those famous harms stem not from the traits themselves but from rules, stereotypes, demands, and double standards that create, maintain, and enforce certain *connections* among them. To talk about these harms, we'll need vocabulary for *norms* that connect different gendered traits in the collective imagination.

Examples of gender norms include the social demand that members of the category *man* refrain from the behavior of wearing skirts, the collective judgment that body hair (a sexed biological trait) is unsuitable for those in the category *woman*, and the expectation that if someone's sexed biology includes breasts,

DOI: 10.4324/9781003053330-3

it also includes a vulva. What these examples have in common is captured by the following rough definition:

> A gender norm is *a social expectation linking two or more gendered traits, which is considered generally applicable or binding.*

Let's unpack the different parts of our tentative definition.

Gender norms are *expectations*. They may attempt to represent how things are (e.g., a shared belief that women have high-pitched voices) or how things should be (e.g., a societal demand that women speak quietly and laugh at men's jokes). Some have a dual or ambiguous character, involving both a belief-like expectation that two or more gendered characteristics will go together and a desire-like expectation that something has gone wrong if they don't.

Gender norms are *social*. Unlike gender feels, which are features of an individual's psychology and potentially idiosyncratic, gender norms belong to the collective social awareness of (some segment of) a community. Like the rules of chess, the grammar of a language, or the concept of a legislature, they are publicly available conceptual resources, which many individuals can use to make sense of the world around them. But if, say, a single individual thinks of ovaries whenever they see a blue necktie, while their wider community has no sense of a link between these two traits, then that is not a gender norm in our sense.

Gender norms are social in another sense: *they belong to a particular society or community* at a particular time. It is likely that no two human communities maintain precisely the same gender norms, and any given community's norms can change over time. All of our examples of gender norms are specific to some cultural context – usually, but not always, that of the authors – and are not meant to be understood as universal. It is in principle possible that a human society could have *no* gender norms whatsoever (or could limit them to a few highly circumscribed and inoffensive types), although to our knowledge there are no uncontroversial examples of human societies that have in fact done this.[1]

Gender norms are considered *generally applicable and binding*, not as expectations about the traits of a particular individual. A social expectation that some particular man be stoic does not count as a gender norm if people have no impulse to generalize it to other men (e.g., if they expect him to be stoic only because he is a paramedic). This particularity gives us another way to distinguish gender feels from gender norms: feels can link gendered traits in individual, nonbinding ways. Our paramedic might feel that his stoicism is important to his sense of himself as a man without committing himself to the belief that men in general are stoic.

Although they are seen as *generally* applicable, gender norms need not be seen as *universal*. Certain individuals might be regarded as personally exceptional and exempt from some norms, or a norm might be modulated by someone's personal characteristics or group membership. Norms regarding the category *women*, for example, might apply only to women of a particular race, ethnicity, class, caste, age, profession, subculture, body size and type, religion, or (dis)ability status, or women in certain groups might be exempted from them. Expectations about men's and women's sexuality look different for black and white women, for disabled and nondisabled men, and so on. There is no definitive way to cleanly partition the gender system off from the other social systems with which it interacts.

Gender norms link *two or more gendered traits*. This linking might take one of many forms: an expectation that two traits typically coincide, that they don't overlap at all, an expectation that having one of them entails having the other (without any implication in the other direction) or anything else of this sort. A given gender norm might make reference to other socially salient traits like age, class, race, or (dis)ability, but it must also involve at least at least two distinct gendered traits.

The way that gender norms *link* traits is a large part of what makes them morally objectionable. Even if there's nothing wrong with being a man, with a lack of interest in children, or having both traits at once, there is something objectionable about a societal demand that men be uninterested in children and that women take up the slack of child-related care work.

Gender norms are *typically maintained or enforced* by deliberate indoctrination, by unconscious reproduction of stereotypes in our personal lives, by portrayals of gendered life in media, by explicit articulation and endorsement of the norm, by punishments for nonconformity, by rewards for conformity, by treating nonconforming individuals as unimportant or unreal, or in any of a number of other ways. We do not want to say that coercive enforcement is a defining characteristic of gender norms, but it is an incredibly common mechanism for ensuring their persistence.[2] A more complete account of the gender system would probably distinguish gender norms from their enforcement mechanisms; we will leave them in the background and will generally think of gender norms as typically "bringing them along".

While we stop short of categorically condemning all gender norms, we think that most of them deserve feminist suspicion, both because they stunt and circumscribe our development as human beings, and because their enforcement mechanisms cause needless harm.

Just as we classified gender feels by classifying the traits they were about, so we can classify gender norms by classifying the traits they connect. For instance, the expectation that women (and only women) should wear lipstick is a category-behavior norm, since it connects a gender category (woman) with a gendered behavior (wearing lipstick). The expectation that people with breasts also have vulvas is a biology norm, since it connects one aspect of sexed biology to another.

This way of dividing up norms is helpful because different kinds of norms turn out to be responsible for different kinds of sexist harms, enforced and maintained by different mechanisms, and challenged by different activist traditions.

3.1.1 Category-Behavior Norms

Category-behavior norms push people into performing separate social roles, which are typically unequal, on the basis of their gender category membership. Examples include "pink is for girls and not boys", "women are bad at math", "nonbinary folks dye their hair unnatural colors", "long hair is not normal/proper for men", "being the primary caregiver of one's children is unmanly", "men are assertive", "(white) women are sensitive and need protection", "nonbinary folks wear pronoun pins", and "boys like to play with toy guns".

As our examples might indicate, category-behavior norms are a major locus of traditional sexism. Anyone who believes in the equality of women, men, and others (that they should generally be afforded the same opportunities, be treated with the same respect, and be understood as having about the same range of dispositions and capacities) should be suspicious of category-behavior norms. Accordingly, many forms of feminism default to opposing these norms, although they may carve out some exceptions (e.g., for norms that serve some role in remediating gender inequality). This is not by any means universal: some feminists, like Gilligan (1982), Chodorow (1989), and Daly (1990), accept certain category-behavior norms and instead focus their criticism on the devaluation of behaviors associated with the category *woman*.

Category-behavior norms are also implicated in some forms of gatekeeping of trans legitimacy ("How can you expect us to believe you're a woman if you can't be bothered to act like one?") and in other social harms to queer and gender-nonconforming people. Enforcement of category-behavior norms involves punishing gender nonconformity; examples include "corrective" rape of queer women (or queer people perceived to be women), bullying effeminate men or butch women, and denying a trans man legal or social recognition as a man because he wears nail polish.[3] Liberatory trans and queer activism are therefore typically hostile to category-behavior norms.

In the authors' main cultural context, the most common category-behavior norms involve the categories *woman* and *man*, although a variety of stereotypes about nonbinary identities are also emerging.[4] In societies with longer traditions of recognizing other gender categories, there may be other category-behavior norms. For example, if *burrnesha* is a gender category in the traditional Albanian context, "burrneshas must not marry" and "burrneshas may smoke" would be category-behavior norms in that context.

What would a society without category-behavior norms look like? It would recognize that there is no right or wrong way to be a woman or a man or both or neither. It would not demand that anyone do certain tasks or pursue certain interests based on their gender category membership, nor would it exclude them from activities on that basis. In such a society, gender category membership would not count for much of anything in our day-to-day social interactions. Such a society might still be unjust in other ways – for instance, it might deny some trans and intersex[5] people's claims on gender category membership based on their sexed biology or make the legitimacy of such claims contingent on medical interventions (e.g., by making genital surgery a prerequisite for changing the gender markers on one's identity documents). That is, it might have category-biology norms and treat its gender categories as "biological sexes", though ones mercifully divested of other sorts of gendered baggage.

3.1.2 Category-Biology Norms

Category-biology norms make it easy to sort people into gender categories, which can then be used to regulate their behavior.

Examples include "women ovulate", "men don't have breasts", "women don't have beards", "normal/healthy women have serum testosterone levels below 5 nmol/L", "anyone with a penis is a man", "men are typically taller and more muscular than women", and "streak gonads are an intersex trait".

The most conspicuous harms of category-biology norms affect trans and intersex people by denying them appropriate category recognition based on their biology or by demanding that biology must be changed to "match" one's category. But anyone whose biology is deemed to be "out of spec" for their category can be adversely affected: for example, men deemed physically weak, hirsute women, and men with gynecomastia all experience social stigma for their failure to conform to category-biology norms.

Common enforcement mechanisms for category-biology norms include refusal to recognize category membership and pressure or coercion to change one's body. More specifically, they include legal and institutional refusal to allow trans people to change our gender-category-of-record without undergoing specific medical interventions, the type of violence against trans women that Bettcher (2014) refers to as "reality enforcement", erasure of transmasculine experience by insisting that only women menstruate, shaming of men with an "unmanly" lack of upper body strength, social expectations that women with facial hair must remove or obfuscate it at any cost (while men are permitted to grow beards), pathologization of breast growth in men (but not in women) as "gynecomastia", nonconsensual surgery to "correct" the genitals of intersex infants and young people (Human Rights Watch, 2017), deeming nonstereotypical height in adolescent girls to be pathologically "excessive" and promoting growth attenuation interventions to "treat" it (Louhiala, 2007), and media portrayals that foreground women with stereotypically feminine bodies and men with stereotypically masculine bodies while others are either ignored or presented as freakish.

Rejection of category-biology norms – or at least of most of the mainstream ones – is an important theme in most strands of trans and intersex activism. Both of these activist communities typically object to physiological prerequisites for recognized membership in the *woman* and *man* categories and to pressure to alter one's biology to conform to expectations for one's category. Some category-biology norms, such as expectations that women should not have "too much" body hair or physical strength, have also been important targets of other strands of feminist and body-acceptance activism.

In a society without category-biology norms, it would be understood that men can have all kinds of bodies, and that women can as well. No one would throw prenatal "gender reveal" parties[6] or say "it's a girl!" or "it's a boy!" after inspecting a newborn's genitals. There would be no social expectation that trans people must undergo certain medical interventions in order to "count" as members of our categories, and medical interventions on intersex infants would not be justified by the idea that a child must be surgically made into a member of a particular category. There could still be norms linking biological traits to each other, which might stigmatize those with "abnormal" or "incongruous" bodies, but none of this would be understood in terms of what sort of biology is specifically appropriate to a "woman" or a "man".

A society without category-biology norms might still have category-behavior norms, and with different behaviors considered appropriate for women versus men, but one's place in this system would not be determined based on anything about one's biology (instead, category membership might be freely chosen by individuals or assigned by some biology-independent random process). Khader (2018, p. 103) suggests that some Native American and African cultures furnish real examples of such societies, citing evidence from Smith (2010) and Amadiume (1997).

3.1.3 Biology-Behavior Norms

Biology-behavior norms are obviously unjust, in ways that feminists and trans activists have noticed. They play a role in traditional sexism, where unchosen features of someone's biology, discerned by a ritual of infant (or prenatal) genital inspection, commit them to performing certain behaviors (like military service or housework) and exclude them from performing others. They also play a role in medical gatekeeping, where a trans person's access to hormones or surgery is made contingent on behaviors that are linked to biology only by culturally arbitrary stereotypes. Why should the lives of men, women, and nonbinary people be constrained in these ways? Shouldn't everyone be free to mix and match biology and behaviors as they see fit, without regard for anyone else's narrow preconceptions?

Although biology-behavior norms are a core area of feminist interest, clear-cut examples of *direct* biology-behavior norms are rare. Most biology-behavior norms are mediated by categories, as compositions of category-biology and category-behavior norms. There might be an emergent cultural expectation that, on average, people with breasts are bad at math, but for most purposes this is probably best understood in terms of a category-biology norm ("women have breasts and men don't") plus a category-behavior norm ("women are bad at math"). And although some mental health professionals might refuse to sign off on a trans woman's vaginoplasty if she doesn't wear makeup, this might be best analyzed in terms of an understanding that makeup is evidence of womanhood (or suitability for womanhood), plus the idea that only women ought to have vaginas.

Nevertheless, there are a few plausible examples of relatively direct biology-behavior norms. Some of these are innocuous biomedical guidelines or expectations, like the expectation that people with prostates (biology) ought to get prostate cancer screenings (a behavior), provided they are over 50.[7] Likewise, we understand (correctly) that the behavior of ear piercing typically results in having pierced ears (biology) and that the behavior of taking testosterone often results in increased body hair growth (biology).

There are also some arguable examples of other, more problematic sorts of biology-behavior norms. These include identification of testicles (biology) with bold and courageous behavior, cutting out explicit mention of categories in favor of a more direct connection. Similarly, the misogynistic expectation that people with menstrual cycles (biology) are especially mentally unstable, and so cannot be trusted with important decisions (behavior), appeals directly to biology to justify expectations about behavior, although the motivation typically involves attitudes about *women* (a category).[8]

Other plausible examples of implicit biology-behavior norms can be found in various design, engineering, and architectural decisions. Criado Perez (2019) documents many such examples: "one-size-fits-all" products and "standard weights" designed for body sizes that are more typical for men than women; "unisex" bathrooms with urinals but without disposal bins for sanitary products; workplaces designed with the expectation that none of the employees will be pregnant.[9] If certain ways of arranging the workplace (behavior) place essential items on shelves too high for many people in the stereotypically female height range (biology) to reach, this enforces a biology-behavior norm.

Exactly which biology-behavior norms are innocuous, and which are pernicious, is a matter of substantive debate. Most of us grant that some aspects of medical practice ought to be contingent on biology (people without testicles needn't check themselves for signs of testicular cancer), but many strands of feminist thought would go farther by, for example, arguing that because of the asymmetrical risks and costs of pregnancy, we are justified in associating physiological pregnancy liability with various social behavior that offer some material accommodation and compensation beyond the narrowly medical context.[10]

What would a society without biology-behavior norms look like? If only *direct* biology-behavior norms were selectively expunged, the resulting social order might not look all that different, but to really eliminate biology-behavior norms, one would need to disrupt the way that category-biology and category-behavior norms together give rise to biology-behavior norms. This could be done by eliminating category-biology norms, category-behavior norms, or both, or possibly by disrupting the system of norms and categories in subtler or more complex ways.

3.1.4 Category Norms

The three pairings just discussed represent many of the most obvious issues in the gender system, but they do not exhaust the space of possible norms. There are also norms linking different traits from the same bucket; category norms provide some of the most accessible examples.

Consider Dembroff's (2020) description of the "binary axis", according to which "The genders *men* and *women* are binary, discrete, immutable, exclusive, and exhaustive". This description packs in a whole range of norms: that if someone belongs to the category *woman*, they do not belong to the category *man*, that any adult who is not a woman must be a man, that no one goes from being a woman to being a man, and so on. Another example of a category norm is the invalidating assumption that nonbinary people are all *really* women or girls.

Category norms are prominently implicated in the erasure and marginalization of anyone who is not easily sorted into one of the commonly recognized categories, including nonbinary/genderqueer people and some intersex people. Enforcement mechanisms include the use of cover terms like "ladies and gentlemen" or "boys and girls", the requirement to check either the "M" or the "F" box on various official forms, and the segregation of facilities like restrooms and fitting rooms into "women's" and "men's" options, especially when neutral alternatives are not provided or are not easily accessible.

Nonbinary/genderqueer activism and related strands of trans and queer activism have prominently targeted these category norms. Some work related to intersex politics (e.g., Fausto-Sterling, 2000; Holmes, 2008; Costello, 2020) and some attempts to problematize the gender binary as a specifically modern Western innovation (e.g., Lugones, 2007) also target these norms (among others).

What would a society without category norms look like? If standard cissexist and patriarchal category-biology and category-behavior norms were present in full force, then eliminating direct category norms might not change much. A society could recognize the possibility of someone being neither a woman nor a man (or both a woman and a man) in principle, but if it insisted on permanently sorting the vast majority of people into one or the other of these categories based on their physiology at birth, then this possibility might not have much practical impact on most people's lives. Insofar as categories play an important role in mediating biology or behavior norms (discussed in the following), the disruption of category norms might help to disrupt these other norms as well. Eliminating or curtailing category norms is an important component of the program of legitimizing and respecting agender, bigender, and genderfluid people (among others), but to make real progress in this area, we must address various norms involving categories, not just the ones that directly link categories to each other.

3.1.5 Biology Norms

Most societies, including our own, expect that certain biological traits will go together (such as vulvas and the capacity to give birth) or will *not* go together (such as breasts and a penis). These expectations are biology norms. They often go beyond acknowledging the existence of statistical correlations and manifest as assumptions that these correlations are exceptionless, that they *ought to* obtain or that bodies presenting counterexamples to them are marginal, impossible, incongruous, defective, disordered, or disgusting.

Like biology-behavior norms, biology norms are often mediated by gender categories: vulvas and fertility are assumed to go together because both are considered part of what it is to be a *woman* or to have a normal *female* body. The harms and enforcement mechanisms of biology norms should be familiar from our discussion category-biology norms: medical interventions to "correct" certain intersex combinations of biological traits, gatekeeping rules that make access to one body modification contingent on having had another, cultural representations of bodies that violate the relevant norms as revolting or defective, and the targeting of such bodies for discrimination and violence.

What would a society without biology norms look like? It probably would, and should, include a scientific community that believed many nonjudgmental statistical generalizations about sexed biology. To expect otherwise would be to expect either willful ignorance of certain empirical facts (which we take to be both unlikely and desirable) or very different empirical facts brought about by the use of medical technologies (which is an interesting speculative possibility, but not one we have much to say about). But our hypothetical society could embrace these generalizations without giving them a status that deserved the name of "norms". It would not regard bodies with rare or "unnatural" combinations of biological traits as obviously disordered or disgusting and would not seek to eliminate or prevent them by promotion or restriction of medical interventions. In order to keep pernicious biology norms from arising indirectly, the society would need to limit its biology-category norms to ensure that they didn't give rise to biology norms linking different biological traits associated with the same category.

3.1.6 Behavior Norms

If category-behavior norms sort people into (typically) two discrete behavioral boxes, behavior norms create those boxes in the first place. It's surprisingly hard to think of behavior norms that are not mediated by gender categories, but here is one possible class of examples: above and beyond the baseline discrimination faced by women in fields like academic philosophy, engineering, or law, it might be that women (or others) with a hyperfeminine aesthetic or affect are *especially* unlikely to be taken seriously in these fields. These cases might involve norms like "lawyers don't wear dresses and bright lipstick", which make no direct reference to gender categories.

But these examples still seem to involve tacit reference to gender categories (consider how easy it is to describe the behaviors in question as "feminine"). Clear examples of pure behavior norms are hard to find.

3.1.7 Category-Biology-Behavior Norms

Since gender norms connect traits, any given norm must be about at least two traits. But there is no reason to think that two is the upper limit. A norm that involved traits from all three of our buckets would be a category-biology-behavior norm.

One plausible example is "women with breasts ought to wear a bra", which makes essential reference to the behavior of wearing a bra, the category *woman* (since it does not apply to men with breasts) and the biological feature *breasts* (since it does not apply to women without them). Similarly, some modes of dress (a behavior) may be regarded as specific to women (a category) and inappropriately sexual or unflattering on some women based on gender-laden differences in their body types (biology). Some previously mentioned norms might also be better analyzed as category-biology-behavior norms. For example, perhaps the biology-behavior norm "courage resides in the testicles" is better understood as the category-laden variant "*men's* courage resides in their testicles", or perhaps both interpretations are useful in different ways.

3.2 "Destroy All Gender!"

In some queer and feminist circles, it's popular to argue that "gender" is pernicious: that it harms women (and possibly others) and that, if possible, it would be desirable to abolish or drastically curtail it.

In the Anglophone political discourse of the moment, the anti-"gender" position has become closely associated with ostensibly feminist arguments for transphobic and trans-exclusionary positions, which often brand themselves as "gender critical". But superficially similar rhetoric also has a long history in trans activism, as exemplified by the influential work of Riki Wilchins (2013), Kate Bornstein (1994), and Alyson Escalante (2016), or Tre'vell Anderson's (2021) more recent remark that "gender is a scam". And arguments against "gender", or particular manifestations of it, are commonplace in radical feminist work that is not notably trans-antagonistic or does not engage with trans issues at all. Sally Haslanger (2012) argues for the abolition of the gender categories *woman* and *man*, and Maria Lugones (2007) argues against an arrangement she calls "the colonial/modern gender system", though both note that there could be non-patriarchal ways of organizing something they call "gender".

Looking at all this, one begins to suspect that different self-styled enemies of "gender" have very different targets in mind, and that this vagueness (and the rhetorical legerdemain that it enables) is part of what makes the "gender critical" framing so useful to transphobes. Concerns about such vagueness are nothing new. Julia Serano (2013), for example, notes that vague gender abolitionist ideas can easily slide in transphobic or otherwise counterproductive directions:

> I cannot tell you how many times I have read and heard claims that feminists are trying to "move beyond gender", or to bring on the "end of gender", invoked in attempts to portray trans-sexuality and transgenderism as antithetical to feminism. Here is what I want to know: what exactly is the "end of gender"? What

does it look like? Are there words to describe male and female bodies at the end of gender? Or do we purge all words that refer to male- or female-specific body parts and reproductive functions for fear that they will reinforce gender distinctions? Do we do away with activities such as sports, sewing, shaving, cooking, fixing cars, taking care of children, and of course, man-on-top-woman-on-bottom penetration sex, because these have been too closely associated with traditional masculine and feminine roles in the past?

The problem highlighted by Serano is that condemnation of "gender" potentially means as many different things as "gender" means. Having developed some tools for talking about some of the different things that "gender" can mean, let's see how they help us to navigate some of the equivocations and pseudoconflicts in anti-"gender" rhetoric.

3.2.1 Abolishing Norms

The most compelling case against "gender" is, at its heart, a case against what we have been calling gender norms and especially against (direct or indirect) biology-behavior norms (c.f. Problematic Slogan 1 ("Gender is the social interpretation of sex") and Problematic Slogan 2 ("Gender is an oppressive system that ties certain behaviors and characteristics to sex") from Chapter 1 of this book). Philosopher Rebecca Reilly-Cooper (2016b) provides a convenient recent example of this sort of anti-"gender" argument:

> The solution is to abolish gender altogether. We do not need gender. We would be better off without it. Gender as a hierarchy with two positions operates to naturalise and perpetuate the subordination of female people to male people, and constrains the development of individuals of both sexes.

Reilly-Cooper says this in an attempt to delegitimize nonbinary identities, as part of a larger a trans-antagonistic "gender critical" agenda,[11] but her case against "gender" seems compelling: who could defend a system that does all these things? Note, though, that what is compelling here is the case against certain gender norms, so this is only a case against other things called "gender" to the extent that they are inseparable from those norms.

As we've noted throughout this chapter, gender norms are a significant source of injustice, including traditional sexism and the oppression of trans, queer, and intersex people. From a feminist perspective, (direct or indirect) biology-behavior norms are especially salient: what reasonable, decent person could fail to recognize the injustice of dictating or restricting someone's behavior based on their (often unchosen) biological traits?

It is quite natural and appropriate to conclude that we'd be better off without gender norms altogether. After all, there is little to be said for the expectation that women (and only women) should wear makeup, the demand that men should suppress their emotions, or the belief that girls should be physically smaller and weaker than boys.

Or at least, we'd be better off without *most* gender norms. The overwhelming majority of our readers, including feminists and trans and queer activists of all stripes, would probably grant that *some* gender norms are inoffensive or even desirable. Here are a few that are widely (though presumably not universally) accepted:

> "People who are considering getting pregnant should have blood folate levels of at least 7 nmol/L" (a biology norm).

> "Generally speaking, an adult with a cervix should get cervical cancer screenings every few years" (a biology-behavior norm).

> "If someone is publicly known to be a man, then, in the absence of extenuating circumstances, it is appropriate to use the word 'man' to talk about him, and to refer to him with such third-person pronouns as 'he' and 'him'"(a category-behavior norm).

So the view that *all* gender norms should be opposed is uncommon, even in radical queer and feminist circles. But if some relatively circumscribed class of necessary or harmless norms is exempted, many of us would say that *all other gender norms* are in some sense bad news, or perhaps go so far as to say that they ought to be opposed or abolished, at least as an ideal or an aspiration. (See Khader (2018) for concerns about trying to realize this ideal in the actual world, particularly Chapters 4 and 5.)

Not all authors explicitly acknowledge such more-or-less acceptable norms, but those who do may hold that they are not, strictly speaking, "gender"[12] or that, if freed from the other norms, they would be a new and different kind of "gender".[13] These types of framings make it possible to recognize this issue while maintaining something recognizably akin to an anti-"gender" rhetorical position.

Another possibility for rehabilitating gender norms is to get rid of coercive enforcement mechanisms, and adopt something more like genre conventions, so that "women wear nail polish" is a norm on the order of "science fiction stories incorporate spacecraft". No one enforces a requirement that science fiction stories incorporate spacecraft, and some science fiction stories may violate the usual expectations. A story might bend the conventions of science fiction, blend genres, or just be hard to classify. If the norms surrounding gender were like this, instead of being coercively enforced, they would certainly be less objectionable.[14]

As things stand now, many gender norms seem worthy of our feminist condemnation. It might be that removing certain problematic norms is not currently practical or even possible, or that the wrong selective removal of norms might do more harm than good, but none of this show these norms in an especially positive light. And it might be possible to rehabilitate norms as something more like genre conventions, but this would require a significant overhaul of the current system.

If we understand "gender" as a system of norms, then there's a cogent (though not airtight) case against "gender". But many anti-"gender" authors go further.

3.2.2 Abolishing Behaviors: "Throw Your Makeup in the Bin"

Some authors go beyond feminist critique of gender norms and the coercive mechanisms used to enforce them and direct their critique at gendered behaviors. Bindel (2019), a columnist in the UK's *Independent*, rightly points out that many women experience social pressure to wear makeup and that this pressure is bad. But she concludes that wearing makeup is bad:

> Do yourself a favour, and throw your makeup in the bin. It would be a much more revolutionary act than burning your bra.

Rachel Ivey (2015), of the militant radical ecofeminist organization Deep Green Resistance, observes that women are subordinated but then uses this as evidence for the claim that trans people, especially trans women, are "actually just reinforcing . . . stereotypes". Ivey doesn't distinguish between norms, gender categories, gendered behaviors, and gender feels, but some of her ire is clearly directed at behaviors deemed feminine.

> It's not a coincidence that 91% of those who are raped are female, and 99% of the perpetrators are male. It's not a coincidence that the shoes make it hard to run away.

Bindel and Ivey seem to have gone beyond critique of compulsory femininity and jumped to the conclusion that no woman in her right mind would have anything to do with feminine behaviors except as a result of the pressure of the relevant norms, and the voice of any woman who protests that she sincerely wants to involve herself in any of them can be dismissed as a symptom of patriarchal brainwashing. But the fact that no one should be coerced into wearing makeup or high heels does not, by itself, tell us whether there is anything wrong with anyone's choosing to.

A behavior need not be inherently oppressive to figure in oppressive norms. Some behaviors, such as child care or lifting heavy objects, are valuable contributions to society, regulated by norms that enforce gendered oppression through division of labor. Others, like tattoos with gendered significance, are expressions of individual freedom that are neither intrinsically morally good nor intrinsically morally bad but may be governed by coercive practices. There might be *some* behaviors that are bad for society overall or so bad for their participants that few people would want to participate in them unless subjected to overwhelming social pressure. But if so, they are bad on their own merits and not in virtue of their being part of "gender".

When evaluating claims that a behavior is bad, we should moreover be wary of double standards. Serano (2007, Ch. 7) reminds us that traits deemed "feminine" are often seen as worse and more artificial than those deemed "masculine" – an evaluative belief that many feminists have uncritically absorbed. Narayan (2019) and Khader (2018) remind us that the behaviors of women from the global south often receive disproportionate criticism from the global north. And trans people frequently report being criticized for behaviors that pass unnoticed when cis people engage in them.

3.2.3 Abolishing Gender Categories: A World Without Women?

A more interesting kind of project seeks to generalize a case against (certain) gender norms into a case for the abolition of (certain) gender categories. For example, Sally Haslanger (2012, p. 8) writes:

> Roughly, women are those subordinated in a society due to their perceived or imagined female reproductive capacities. It follows that in societies where being (or presumed to be) female does not result in subordination along any dimension, there are no women. Moreover, justice requires that where there is such subordination, we should change social relations so there will be no

more women (or men). (This will not require mass femicide! Males and females may remain even where there are no men or women.)

For Haslanger, doing away with unjust norms entails emptying out the *woman* and *man* categories (though it allows for the possibility of other gender categories). Haslanger's focus is on unjust biology-behavior norms, and so, in the language of our framework, the motivating concern can be understood in terms of the role that gender categories play in mediating those norms.[15]

It is obvious that the step from "these norms are incompatible with the demands of justice" to "the categories that participate in these norms are incompatible with the demands of justice" is not formally valid. It goes through only if gender categories and gender norms are inseparable – if, for example, the categories cannot exist without their unjust norms, or eliminating the categories is the only way (or at least the best way) of disrupting the norms that they mediate.

So are gender categories inseparable from unjust norms, and if so, *which norms*? Unfortunately, there is little agreement, either among philosophers or among the general public. The popular naïve cissexist view holds that one's gender category membership is fully determined by one's sexed biology, so that gender categories can survive the abolition of all category-behavior norms, but certain category-biology norms will persist as long as the categories do. Another naïve view holds that gender categories are "gender roles", understood, variously, as bundles of norms that tend to be applied to the same people, bundles of behaviors prescribed by those norms, or some combination of these. On this alternative view, category-behavior norms are ineliminable as long as gender categories remain, but any category-biology norms can be destroyed while leaving the categories intact.

Philosophers defend various more sophisticated analyses of gender categories and category membership, which appeal to complex combinations of traits, norms, and feels. McKitrick (2015) analyzes category membership in terms of behavior-feels and dispositions to engage in gendered behaviors. If we eliminated category-behavior norms, would gender categories as McKitrick sees them still exist? Other authors (Daly, 2017; Corvino, 2000; Hale, 1996; Stoljar, 1995) characterize manhood and womanhood as cluster properties made up of sexed biological traits, gendered behaviors, and category-feels. Could such a cluster property survive the elimination of category-biology norms, category-behavior norms, or both? While none of these analyses directly address the question of which changes to our gender norms would suffice for the abolition of gender categories, we see no reason to think that they would agree with each other.

If our main goal is disrupting biology-behavior norms (or at least the ones mediated by categories), it's enough to remove category-behavior norms, category-biology norms, or both. This *might* turn out to be enough to destroy the gender categories, either because those categories are metaphysically dependent on traditional sexism or cissexism or because as a sociological matter, removing gender norms will cause people to lose interest in the categories until they naturally fade away. But it's far from obvious that it will be enough.

Is there any reason for feminist, queer, and trans activists to aim directly at the destruction of gender categories? One possible rationale is that categories are only *good for* mediating norms, either in the sense this is their only practical role or in the sense that the only theoretical use for thinking about categories is to critique norms. Both versions of the thought might seem tempting at first – after all, some putative roles for gender categories, like keeping track of people's genital status, look morally dubious, and some putative roles for gender-category concepts, like describing biological essences, look scientifically dubious – but both versions overlook at least one important source of categories' significance.

Gender categories play a valuable role in the way many people, including many trans and queer people, see themselves and each other. Like Ada, Blaise, and Cass, many of us seem to care about our category membership in ways that go beyond simple norm-driven benefits in terms of what membership in a particular category allows us to do under the prevailing patriarchal social order. Cull (2019) argues that abolishing gender categories would deprive trans people of something important by misgendering trans women and trans men, as well as eliminating minority gender categories in non-Western societies. In short, gender categories matter to many people, in a way that can't easily be attributed to their role in mediating gender norms.[16] We'll say more about this mattering, and what it might consist of, in Chapter 4.

To sum up: there is no general consensus on what ways of destroying gender norms would bring about the end of gender categories. So while we haven't ruled out the possibility that widespread societal reforms might destroy some or all of our society's gender categories, it seems premature to treat their destruction as an obvious requirement of the feminist project.

3.3 Alternatives, Loose Ends, and Possible Extensions

We've now filled in all the main moving parts of our theory. Gendered traits can be sorted into three buckets: sexed biology, gendered behavior, and gender categories. Gender norms link traits to one another in the public consciousness, and people have individual feels about their (real or potential) standing in relation to traits.

We can categorize feels and norms according to the traits they're about. This gives us 13 named components: three kinds of traits, three kinds of feels (one about each kind of traits), and seven kinds of norms (one for each set of one or more kinds of traits that can be combined). Some of these components are depicted in Figure 3.1. (To avoid visual clutter, we've omitted depictions of norms that are about only one kind of trait and of norms that are about all three.)

Drawing fine-grained distinctions helps us see that common questions about "gender" (such as whether it is good or bad, and whether it is personal or social) lack well-defined answers and that many arguments and generalizations about "gender" trade on equivocations between conceptually distinct parts of the system.

Ours is not the only possible or useful framework, but we hope that you will find its general approach helpful in conversations about "gender". Even if you disagree with our precise distinctions and terminology, or our specific views on the 13 components we've named, we hope that when you find yourself participating in, or observing, debates about "gender" or "gender identity" or "gender roles", you consider the kinds of questions that our approach suggests. Are all parties to the debate really

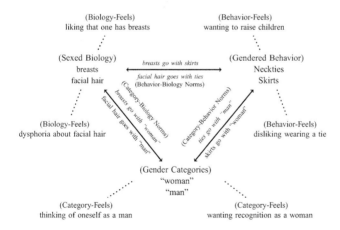

FIGURE 3.1   Three kinds of traits, along with three kinds of feels and three kinds of norms about those traits. (Category norms, biology norms, behavior norms, and category-biology–behavior norms not pictured.)

talking about the same thing? Is someone sliding between different meanings of "gender" to make inferences that are not valid? Are you interpreting others' use of "gender"-related vocabulary in an appropriately nuanced and charitable way?

We hope that some of our specific takeaways are helpful too. We encourage you to distinguish between gendered traits on the one hand and attitudes *about* them (like norms and feels) on the other; to ask whether feels about one trait need to pattern with feels about another; and to notice when someone conflates behaviors or gender categories with the norms that regulate them. We encourage you to borrow our method of categorizing feels and associations based on the traits they are about. This method of categorization has proved useful by helping us name distinctions that were otherwise hard to see (like the difference between category-feels and behavior-feels) and enabling us to make surprising observations about things we'd named (like the observation that category-behavior norms are direct, while biology-behavior norms are typically indirect.)

Before moving on to other topics, we want to briefly consider some alternative approaches and generalizations of our framework.

3.3.1 Comparison With Some Other Approaches

We are not the first to observe the imprecision of the word "gender". As Mari Mikkola (2019) notes at the beginning of her *Stanford Encyclopedia* overview of "Feminist Perspectives on Sex and Gender", "The terms 'sex' and 'gender' mean different things to different feminist theorists and neither are easy or straightforward to characterise". Kate Bornstein (1997, p. 25) playfully offers a simple crossword puzzle where all the clues are different, but the solution is to fill in "gender" for all of them. Brian Earp (2020a, 2020b) argues that the ambiguity of "gender" causes needless confusion in debates about feminism. The ambiguity of existing "gender" talk is recognized across ideological lines; Kathleen Stock (2021, p. 35), whose project is an attack on the politics of trans inclusion and trans liberation, distinguishes four different senses of "gender".

It is not surprising, then, that others have attempted to clarify the issue or to divide up the "gender" space in various ways. In Section 2.4, we saw a common family of approaches that distinguish "gender expression" from "gender identity". Other concepts commonly distinguished from both of these are "sex" (something like our "sexed biology"), "gender role" (some combination of our "gender norms", "gender categories", and "gendered behaviors"), and "gender" (often used as a wastebasket for whatever wasn't covered elsewhere). Such distinctions are useful in many special cases, but are unsystematic, and not nearly as granular as our approach. Most of these components run together multiple things that we have seen reasons to distinguish ("gender identity" encompasses many very different kinds of feels), or are vague in their scope ("gender expression" is sometimes – but only sometimes – treated as including behavior-feels along with behavior), or are have background assumptions built in ("sex" is often taken as packaging our notion of sexed biology with the idea that there are biological "sex categories" that bear an explanatory relation to the various sexed biological traits). Our approach attempts to systematize and clarify the most important insights of this approach while addressing some of the residual ambiguities and presuppositions.

Our distinction between traits and norms is similar to Mikkola's (2011) distinction between descriptive traits (examples include "having ovaries" and "wearing makeup") and evaluative norms (examples include "being feminine"). Unlike us, Mikkola makes no attempt to divide the material traits into anything like behavior and biology – a choice that makes sense in light of Mikkola's emphasis on problematizing the "sex"/"gender" distinction. Our system enables us to recognize socially salient (if fuzzy) distinctions between behavior and biology, as well as corresponding distinctions among feels and associations. (It is unclear how feels and gender categories fit into Mikkola's categorization scheme.)

Haslanger's "focal analysis" of gender (2012, p. 8) distinguishes between "resources" (which would include our "sexed biology" and some of our "gendered behavior"), "gender identity" (which she links to explicit self-understanding, unconscious habits, and internalized societal ideals), and "gender norms". Her taxonomy also explicitly distinguishes some of the social infrastructure that enforces and maintains gender norms: "sex marking & scripts", "gender roles" or "structured patterns of interaction" around work, family, and sex, and "gender symbolism" that includes both images and narratives.

Our approach owes a debt to all of these prior attempts at precisification and seeks to build on them by bringing their insights together. We've tried to consider what happens when we respect all (or almost all) of the implied distinctions and to combinatorially exhaust the ways that they may be crosscutting or may interact. The result is more granular than most other accounts: we have 13 notions of "gender" where most competitors have five or fewer (radical "identity"- or "dysphoria"-splitters like Reed (2012) and R. A. Williams (2019) are notable exceptions), and it offers a degree of systematicity that other approaches lack.

3.3.2 Generalizations and Extensions

We've laid out some useful puzzle pieces that can be used to describe various things that go by the name of "gender". There's still terrain that our theory doesn't cover; in particular, the mechanisms for enforcing gender norms are worthy of their own books. But within the terrain that we do cover, our general taxonomy could be expanded; here are some refinements that might be useful.

3.3.2.1 Recursion

We've allowed for feels about traits but not for feels about feels or about norms.[17] Similarly, we haven't yet considered the possibility of norms that apply to feels or to other norms as well as traits. But certain examples suggest that "higher-order" feels and norms are possible, perhaps even common. A trans-inclusive community might agree that being a man normally involves having category-feels along the lines of "I'm a man" – in other words, the community might endorse a norm linking gender categories to category-feels. A man with no particular personal interest in wearing a dress might still personally resent the expectation that as a man he oughtn't wear one; this would be a feel about norms. A fully worked-out account could use technical tools like recursion to help us characterize infinitely many kinds of potential feels and norms while still ensuring that the characterization was ultimately coherent and well-founded.

3.3.2.2 Starting With More Pieces

We started by dividing traits into three buckets (biology, categories, and behavior) and considered two types of attitudes about the traits (feels and norms). We could have divided up the traits differently (for example, by lumping biology and behavior together into "material traits" or by subdividing biology into separate buckets for hormones, gametes, secondary sexual characteristics, etc.). Each way of sorting traits into buckets would induce corresponding distinctions among feels and norms: we could talk about material-trait-feels or category-gamete norms.

We could also distinguish among different kinds of feels: belief-like versus desire-like states, or conscious versus unconscious attitudes, and so on. Or we could divide norms into institutionally recognized rules versus informal social codes or descriptive expectations whose violation is met with *surprise* versus prescriptive or evaluative expectations whose violations are met with *annoyance, alarm, condemnation,* or *disgust.* These changes would give us more fine-grained ways of distinguishing parts of the gender system built up from the traits: we could speak of belief-like category-feels or institutional behavior norms in the law.

Each of the aforementioned distinctions complicates the picture, but each adds something of value. In general, we would advocate handling them along the lines of our general strategy. First, identify a type of mental or social phenomenon that is *about* some traits. Next, classify instances of this phenomenon according to which traits they're about. Finally, consider how the phenomenon applies to as many types or combinations of traits as possible while noting (and reflecting on) cases where examples are scarce.

3.3.2.3 Feels About Multiple Things

Consider a butch lesbian whose emotional investment in her Carharts and flannel shirts is very much about wearing them *as a woman*; is this a matter of category-feels or behavior-feels? What about a cisgender man with gynecomastia, whose distress at his breasts is specifically distress at being a *man* with breasts; is this a matter of category-feels or biology-feels? Or consider anyone (in any gender category) who specifically delights in the way their twirly dress pairs with their facial hair; is this about behavior-feels or biology-feels?

We've allowed for norms that connect multiple traits, but so far, every example of a gender feel we've considered in detail has been about a single trait. It's possible that an attitude could be irreducibly about multiple traits, like the ones in the previous paragraph – perhaps even arbitrarily many traits. Recognizing this possibility lets us name new, mixed kinds of feels, such as category-behavior feels (for example, wanting to appreciate the beauty of fashion design as a man) or biology-category-behavior feels (for example, a commitment to performing one's own form of womanhood by enhancing one's strong jawline with dramatic makeup).

How we think and feel about one trait is entangled with the other traits that often provide its immediate context. We might feel that one trait flatters or reinforces another or revel in a sense of willful gender-fuckery or transgression. Any gendered behaviors, sexed biological traits, or gender categories may have *personal significance* that allows them to serve as personal invocations or reminders of other traits, and we think that recognizing gender feels about multiple traits is a promising way to represent this kind of personal significance. So although we'll continue to write in terms of behavior-feels, biology-feels, and category-feels, we recognize that the underlying reality is probably more complicated than that.

In the next chapter, we'll have more to say about the personal significance of gender feels. We'll argue that this personal significance cannot be reduced to internalized sexism, and that our default, when assessing whether someone has the gender feels they claim to have, should be to take them at their word.

Notes

1 Oyěwùmí (1997) describes traditional Yorùbá society as genderless, but it may still have gender norms in our sense of the term. Oyěwùmí presents the relevant Yorùbá norms as much more limited than those found in Western/colonial/modern gender systems and as not giving rise to a hierarchical relationship among gender categories. This would make traditional Yorùbá society an important example of the great range of variation in systems of gender norms and of the possibility of a relatively minimal system of gender norms. Some aspects of Oyěwùmí's account are controversial (see, e.g., Bakare-Yusuf, 2003), and a thorough assessment of her claims and analysis would be beyond the scope of this project.

2 Could believing a purely statistical generalization count as endorsing a norm? For example, what if someone thinks men tend to be taller than women on the basis of good evidence and would be disposed to revise this belief if this evidence changed? We don't

think that the individual's belief itself counts as a norm, since norms are shared commitments rather than individual commitments, but the individual's belief might participate in a social norm. Even if the individual treats the generalization as purely statistical, others around them might be subtly enforcing its truth by judging short men and tall women harshly, advocating gendered patterns of medical treatments to "normalize" height, preferring heterosexual pairings where the man is taller than the woman, or making systematic errors that lead them to perceive men as taller and women as shorter than they really are. Norms, as we understand them, involve some societal pressure that makes exceptions marginal – whether by ignoring them, punishing them, devaluing them, or simply rendering them unimaginable.

3 The harms of enforcement do not fall only on notably gender-nonconforming people. Types of enforcement that harm more "typical" people include punishing or shaming a man for "unmanly" displays of emotional vulnerability, refusing to consider a woman for a job operating a turret lathe because it is deemed "men's work", and talking about a hypothetical anesthesiologist with "he" pronouns in an instructional video preparing patients for surgery.

4 These mostly involve expectations of androgyny or of a certain queer-countercultural approach to grooming and attire. See Simmons (2018) for some discussion.

5 Not all intersex people are trans, and not all trans people are intersex, although some people are both trans and intersex. The problems facing the two groups are different (trans people often struggle to access medical treatment that is desired and helpful while intersex people are often coerced into harmful nonconsensual medical treatment) but as our examples throughout this chapter illustrate, gender norms can be harmful to both groups in closely related ways.

6 At least, there would not be the kind of parties familiar from our world, in which a fetus is inferred to be a girl or a boy based on anatomical (or more rarely genetic) evidence. There might in principle be "genital reveal parties", and if the society in question had biology-behavior norms, there might be "gender reveal parties" that didn't use words like "girl" and "boy" but did involve expectations about anticipated hobbies, likes, dislikes, interests, or career choices of an expected child.

7 In the world we inhabit, this expectation is often stated in a way that involves categories like *man*; for example, the American

Cancer Society (2021) recommends that *men* over 50 be screened for prostate cancer. But (like many people invested in trans liberation), we think that it need not and should not be stated in terms of men.

8   It is telling that misogynists are often happy to wield the "menstruation means psychological instability" trope against cisgender women who have not menstruated in some time, as we saw in the rhetoric around the 2016 US presidential election.

9   Criado Perez herself is no friend of trans people, and unfortunately, she frames her observations in needlessly gender-binary terms, but her book nonetheless provides valuable documentation on this point.

10 See, for example, Haslanger (2004).

11 Cf. Allen et al. (2019), Reilly-Cooper (2016a).

12 Oyěwùmí (1997) seems to have something like this in mind when she says that traditional Yorùbá society lacks gender while acknowledging that it has what we would call gender norms.

13 Haslanger (2004, 2012) pursues this approach.

14 For a discussion of gender categories as genre-like, see Temple (2013).

15 We feel compelled to acknowledge that this doesn't fully do justice to the metaphysical nuances of Haslanger's approach. The details are not important for our present purposes, and so we'll leave them aside to avoid getting derailed.

16 Perhaps if we eliminated gender norms, then categories like *woman*, *man*, *nonbinary*, and so on would continue to exist but would cease to count as *gender* categories. (We're not sure; we've deliberately refrained from giving necessary and sufficient conditions for something to count as a gender category or as gendered or from pronouncing on whether there are interesting commonalities among the things that get called "gender".) Would anything desirable be lost if (what are now) gender categories stopped being gender categories and became some other sort of categories instead? We don't think so. Insofar as these categories are valuable, it's not because we use the word "gender" to refer to them, or because that word refers to a unifying and valuable property, but because they enable certain kinds of meaning-making.

17 We suggested in Section 2.1.5 that Jenkins's (2018) theory of gender identity can be fruitfully understood as a theory of category-feels, but it might be more accurately interpreted as a theory of feels about norms or feels involving both categories and norms.

References

Allen, S., Jones, J. C., Lawford-Smith, H., Leng, M., Reilly-Cooper, R., & Stock, K. (2019, May 23). Doing better in arguments about sex, gender, and trans rights. *Medium.* Retrieved September 29, 2021, from https://medium.com/@s.r.allen/doing-better-in-arguments-about-sex-and-gender-f8f02258aff8

Amadiume, I. (1997). *Reinventing Africa: Matriarchy, religion and culture.* Zed Books Ltd. www.jstor.org/stable/1581587?origin=crossref

American Cancer Society. (2021). *American cancer society recommendations for prostate cancer early detection.* www.cancer.org/cancer/prostate-cancer/detection-diagnosis-staging/acs-recommendations.html

Anderson, T. (2021). What does it really mean to be non-binary? *Xtra Magazine.* Retrieved October 11, 2021, from https://xtramagazine.com/culture/what-does-non-binary-mean-194517

Bakare-Yusuf, B. (2003). Yorubas don't do gender. *African Identities, 1,* 121–142.

Bettcher, T. M. (2014). Trapped in the wrong theory: Rethinking trans oppression and resistance. *Signs: Journal of Women in Culture and Society, 39*(2), 383–406. https://doi.org/10.1086/673088

Bindel, J. (2019, January 22). Come on feminists, ditch the makeup bag. It's a far more radical statement than burning your bra. *The Independent.* www.independent.co.uk/voices/makeup-sexist-lipstick-feminism-women-burning-bra-radical-protest-a8740096.html

Bornstein, K. (1994). *Gender outlaw.* Routledge.

Bornstein, K. (1997). *My gender workbook: How to become a real man, a real woman, the real you, or something else entirely.* Routledge.

Chodorow, N. (1989). *Feminism and psychoanalytic theory.* Yale University Press.

Corvino, J. (2000). Analyzing gender. *Southwest Philosophy Review, 17*(1), 173–180. https://doi.org/10.5840/swphilreview200017120

Costello, C. G. (2020). Beyond binary sex and gender ideology. In *The Oxford handbook of the sociology of body and embodiment.* https://doi.org/10.1093/oxfordhb/9780190842475.013.14

Criado Perez, C. (2019). *Invisible women: Data bias in a world designed for men.* Abrams Press.

Cull, M. J. (2019). Against abolition. *Feminist Philosophy Quarterly, 5*(3), Article 3. https://doi.org/10.5206/fpq/2019.3.5898

Daly, H. (2017). Modeling sex/gender. *Think: Philosophy for Everyone, 16*(46), 79–92.

Daly, M. (1990). *Gyn/Ecology: The metaethics of radical feminism*. Beacon Press.

Dembroff, R. (2020). Beyond binary: Genderqueer as critical gender kind. *Philosophers' Imprint, 20*(9), 1–23.

Earp, B. (2020a). What is gender for? *The Philosopher, 108*(2), 94–99.

Earp, B. (2020b). What is your gender? A friendly guide to the public debate. *Practical Ethics*. http://blog.practicalethics.ox.ac.uk/2020/03/what-is-your-gender-a-friendly-guide-to-the-public-debate/

Escalante, A. (2016, June 22). Gender nihilism: An anti-manifesto. *Libcom.Org*. http://libcom.org/library/gender-nihilism-anti-manifesto

Fausto-Sterling, A. (2000). *Sexing the body: Gender politics and the construction of sexuality*. Basic Books.

Gilligan, C. (1982). *In a different voice: Psychological theory and women's development*. Harvard University Press.

Hale, J. (1996). Are lesbians women? *Hypatia, 11*(2).

Haslanger, S. (2004). Future genders? Future races? *Philosophic Exchange, 34*(1), 1–24.

Haslanger, S. (2012). *Resisting reality*. Oxford University Press.

Holmes, M. (2008). *Intersex: A perilous difference*. Rosemont Publishing & Printing Corp.

Human Rights Watch. (2017). *I want to be like nature made me: Medically unnecessary surgeries on intersex children in the US*. https://live-interact-advocates.pantheonsite.io/wp-content/uploads/2017/07/Human-Rights-Watch-interACT-Report-Medically-Unnecessary-Surgeri-on-Intersex-Children-in-the-US.pdf

Ivey, R. (2015, September 16). End of gender: Revolution, not reform. *Medium*. https://medium.com/@deepgreenresist/end-of-gender-revolution-not-reform-cf5f23fd29c7

Jenkins, K. (2018). Toward an account of gender identity. *Ergo: An Open Access Journal of Philosophy, 5*(27). https://doi.org/10.3998/ergo.12405314.0005.027

Khader, S. J. (2018). *Decolonizing universalism: A transnational feminist ethic*. Oxford University Press.

Louhiala, P. (2007). How tall is too tall? On the ethics of oestrogen treatment for tall girls. *Journal of Medical Ethics, 33*(1), 48–50. https://doi.org/10.1136/jme.2006.016253

Lugones, M. (2007). Heterosexualism and the colonial/modern gender system. *Hypatia, 22*(1), 186–219. https://doi.org/10.1111/j.1527-2001.2007.tb01156.x

McKitrick, J. (2015). A dispositional account of gender. *Philosophical Studies, 172*(10), 2575–2589. https://doi.org/10.1007/s11098-014-0425-6

Mikkola, M. (2011). Ontological commitments, sex and gender. In C. Witt (Ed.), *Feminist metaphysics* (pp. 67–83). Springer.

Mikkola, M. (2019). Feminist perspectives on sex and gender. In *Stanford encyclopedia of philosophy*. https://plato.stanford.edu/entries/feminism-gender/

Narayan, U. (2019). Sisterhood and "doing good": Asymmetries of western feminist location, access and orbits of concern. *Feminist Philosophy Quarterly, 5*(2), Article 2. https://doi.org/10.5206/fpq/2019.2.7299

Oyěwùmí, O. (1997). *The invention of women: Making an African sense of western gender discourses*. University of Minnesota Press.

Reed, N. (2012, May 1). Different dysphorias and esoteric embodiments. *Sincerely, Natalie Reed*. https://web.archive.org/web/20121124202952/http://freethoughtblogs.com/nataliereed/2012/05/01/different-dysphorias-and-esoteric-embodiments/

Reilly-Cooper, R. (2016a, May 13). Why self-identification shouldn't be the only thing that defines our gender. *The Conversation*. http://theconversation.com/why-self-identification-shouldnt-be-the-only-thing-that-defines-our-gender-57924

Reilly-Cooper, R. (2016b, June 28). Gender is not a spectrum. *Aeon*. https://aeon.co/essays/the-idea-that-gender-is-a-spectrum-is-a-new-gender-prison

Roman, A. (2019, September 11). *Gender desire vs. gender identity*. https://medium.com/@kemenatan/gender-desire-vs-gender-identity-a334cb4eeec5

Serano, J. (2007). *Whipping girl: A transsexual woman on sexism and the scapegoating of femininity*. Seal Press.

Serano, J. (2013). *Excluded: Making feminist and queer movements more inclusive*. Seal Press.

Simmons, T. (2018). Gender isn't a haircut: How representation of nonbinary people of color requires more than White androgyny. *Color Bloq*. www.colorbloq.org/article/gender-isnt-a-haircut-how-representation-of-nonbinary-people-of-color-requires-more-than-white-androgyny

Smith, A. (2010). Queer theory and native studies: The heteronormativity of settler colonialism. *GLQ: A Journal of Lesbian and Gay Studies, 16*(1–2), 41–68. https://doi.org/10.1215/10642684-2009-012

Stock, K. (2021). *Material girls: Why reality matters for feminism*. Fleet.

Stoljar, N. (1995). Essence, identity, and the concept of woman. *Philosophical Topics*, *23*, 261–293.

Temple, A. (2013, July 29). I'm a trans composer. What the hell does that mean? *NewMusicBox*. https://nmbx.newmusicusa.org/im-a-trans-composer-what-the-hell-does-that-mean/

Wilchins, R. (2013). *Read my lips: Sexual subversion and the end of gender*. Magnus Books.

Williams, R. A. (2019, October 23). The whole "do you need dysphoria to be trans" discourse kind of bothers me because it always assumes that dysphoria is strictly about the body. But there's also: -Gender role dysphoria -Pronoun dysphoria -Name dysphoria -Social dysphoria -Legal dysphoria -Expression dysphoria [Tweet]. *@rach_a_williams*. https://twitter.com/rach_a_williams/status/1186855503126814720

4

"ABOVE ALL THAT"

Glorifying Indifference

4.1 Introduction

One common way to delegitimize trans people's needs is to dismiss our gender feels as confused, incoherent, pernicious, mistaken, ideological, or driven by sinister ulterior motives. Often, these dismissals come with a perception that trans people's reports of our gender feels are misrepresentations of our own mental states and thought processes (though whether these misrepresentations are said to spring from error or deception varies from interpreter to interpreter).

These dismissals include psychologist Ray Blanchard's insistence that it's typical for trans women to transition as a means to some sexual end (Blanchard, 1989; see Serano, 2010, 2020a, 2020b for critique), OB/GYN Lisa Littman's hypothesis that increasing numbers of young transmasculine people are impressionable girls misled by internet trends (Littman, 2018, see Ashley, 2020 and Restar, 2020 for critique), Janice Raymond's accusation that trans women are men who seek to objectify women's bodies and infiltrate women's spaces (Raymond, 1994, see Riddell, 1980 and Stone, 1992 for critique), the oft-repeated view that trans people are transitioning because we somehow aren't aware that it's possible to be gay, and unsolicited reminders from well-meaning cis people that it's possible to be a feminine woman or a masculine man (directed at trans people who are presumed to think otherwise).

DOI: 10.4324/9781003053330-4

In this chapter, we'll lay out some of our reasons for taking trans people's (and everyone else's) self-reported gender feels seriously. By default, one should assume that gender feels are individually variable, that there's nothing wrong with having them, and that when people tell us about their own gender feels (and about how these gender feels relate to their other beliefs or political commitments), we ought to take them at their word. Someone who wants to depart from these defaults in a particular case needs a positive reason for doing so.

Of course, those who refuse to take trans people's gender feels seriously often believe, either implicitly or explicitly, that there are positive reasons for doubt. But when we try to reconstruct these reasons for doubt as arguments, they're not very promising: they don't seem to proceed from true premises by valid inference patterns. So why do so many people continue to find them persuasive? Part of the reason is simple unfamiliarity: if you can't relate to another person's feels, and you don't regularly encounter accurate representations of them, it's tempting to explain them away in terms of errors or ulterior motives. But another relevant factor is ideology: our culture furnishes us with a lot of questionable assumptions about which feels can be taken for granted as typical or reasonable and which need to be explained away. We unpack some of those assumptions in Section 4.3.

4.2 Taking Feels Seriously

When someone reports a particular gender feel (for instance, that they enjoy wearing lipstick or that they don't want to be classified as a woman), our default presumption should be to take them seriously in at least four senses.

1   We should assume that they are *sincere* rather than lying or being manipulative.
2   We should assume that they are *competent* to understand and report their own feels.

3 We should assume that the feels they report are *coherent* – that is, in the absence of evidence to the contrary, we should try to inhabit a perspective from which their reports make sense, and we should not assume that what they are saying is logically inconsistent.

4 We should start from a place of *moral respect* and treat them as they want to be treated in light of their feels, insofar as that's compatible with our other moral values.

We think that people often unjustifiably refuse to take trans people's gender feels seriously in all four ways, but our discussion in this chapter will focus mainly on the first three.

Why should we take trans people's gender feels seriously? Not because there is anything morally distinctive about *gender* feels, but because our default presumption should be (and typically is) to take one another's inner lives seriously. That's not to say that principles 1–4 are without exceptions; sometimes, we have positive reasons to think that someone is insincere, unreflective, confused, or morally mistaken. But they are good defaults that apply in the absence of positive reasons for doubt, and this applies just as much to trans people's gender feels as to other emotional states.

Consider the first two ways of taking feels seriously: assuming people are sincere and competent to report their feels. These presumptions are just instances of our typical approach to introspective testimony, especially when it comes to individual likes, dislikes, and feelings. One plausible reason for this presumption is epistemic: tastes and perspectives vary widely, so we can't reliably discover what others want by generalizing from our own tastes and perspectives, or trying to imagine what a default human being would want. Introspective testimony may be fallible, but it's often the best guide to other people's mental states we have – certainly better than the speculation of outsiders.

Another plausible reason for these presumptions is ethical. Bettcher (2009), along with authors like McGeer (2008) and

Moran (2001), argues that treating someone as authoritative about their thoughts and feelings is a way of acknowledging their ownership of their own thoughts and feelings and perhaps their interpretive authority to decide what those thoughts and feelings amount to.

No matter what the source of our presumptions of sincerity and competence, these presumptions apply to trans people's gender feels just as much as they apply to other mental states. When someone tells us what they want for lunch, or which nickname they prefer to be called by, we default to taking them at their word, unless we have a specific reason not to. When a cisgender man asserts that he believes himself to be a man, or says he likes his beard on an aesthetic level, we're generally happy to leave it at that, without inventing elaborate, vaguely sinister explanations. Taking trans people's gender feels seriously, in the sense of treating their testimony as sincere and competent, is just another application of our usual default presumptions about introspective testimony.

Likewise, taking trans people's gender feels seriously in the third sense, by presuming coherence, is an instance of a common and reasonable default presumption about feels. We know that human tastes can vary widely without anyone's being wrong. Lots of things are worth liking, and it is generally good practice to exercise humility about the limitations of one's own perspective and imagination. If it's hard to imagine how anyone could want something you personally abominate (like the taste of durian or the pitter-patter of little feet), this is typically evidence of your lack of imagination rather than the incoherence of other people's desires. The world is a big place, and people are into all kinds of things.

Finally, we should default to treating trans people's feels with moral respect because that's how we should presumptively treat everyone's values and preferences. True, the presumption of respect can be overridden by other moral values, like harm prevention; the suffering of factory-farmed pigs might override any presumption that we should respect your pro-bacon feels, and women's need for bodily autonomy overrides any presumption that we should respect heterosexual men's desire to grope them (regardless of whether this attachment to groping counts as a gender feel). But in a free and pluralistic society, people must be given the freedom to pursue their own life plans and projects, so long as they're not imposing unacceptable costs on others. Deciding when a cost is unacceptable is outside the scope of our project, but it's not enough to appeal to a knee-jerk sense of discomfort or the vague sense that what someone else values is decadent or frivolous.

All of the presumptions 1–4 are defaults that can be overridden if we have evidence that the speaker is lying, incompetent, confused, or malicious. But many decisions to withhold moral respect from trans people do not meet this evidential standard; a knee-jerk "how could anyone in their right mind want *that*!?" reaction is not enough.

If trans people's gender feels were judged by the same standards as other kinds of feels, they would be taken more seriously than they currently are. Of course, someone could respond to this observation by looking for special reasons to dismiss trans people's gender feels or by taking all feels less seriously. But we think there are independent reasons for rejecting these options and taking trans people's gender feels seriously. Both authors have spent time in subcultural spaces that value and support a diversity of gender feels, and, for the most part, these spaces work well: the freedom to explore and experiment is widely beneficial (Ashley, 2019b), and hypothetical risks or adverse effects either fail to materialize (Schilt & Westbrook, 2015) or are rare enough to fall within our general collective tolerance for freedom bringing risk (Wiepjes et al., 2018; Narayan et al., 2021) or are attributable not to the freedom to act on one's gender-feels but to transphobic backlash (Wilson et al., 2016; Veale et al., 2017).

So taking feels seriously is the right default position. Defaults can be overridden by a good enough reason, but common reasons for discounting trans gender feels turn out to be bad reasons when spelled out explicitly. In the next section, we turn to the task of spelling them out.

4.3 Why *Wouldn't* You Take Feels Seriously?

Different kinds of gender feels are targets for different kinds of dismissal. In the case of biology-feels, a common presumption is that caring about one's physical form is vain, shallow, or otherwise wrong. In the case of behavior-feels, legitimate feminist criticisms of gender norms are sometimes overextended to sexist dismissals of feminine-coded behaviors and positive feels about them. Dismissals of category-feels often rely on the assumption that gender categories are good only for mediating biology-behavior norms and so could not provoke any reasonable emotional investment on their own. We devote one subsection to each type of dismissal.

4.3.1 We're Not Supposed to Care About Our Bodies

Trans people's biology-feels, like trans people's bodies, are often subject to intense scrutiny and questioning. Trans men with breasts often want to get rid of them; critics delegitimize this desire by claiming that it's the result of patriarchal brainwashing. Trans women often want bigger breasts; critics delegitimize this desire by claiming that it's the result of sexual perversion. What legitimate reason, cis people sometimes demand to know, could trans people have for caring about the shapes of their bodies at all? This skepticism about our biology-feels sometimes spills over to feels about behaviors that are closely connected to our bodies (such as choices in hairstyle, makeup, or clothing).

Cis people are the targets of similar prejudices (though not always to the same degree). A cis woman's desire for breast implants may be dismissed as shallow, vain, or foolish while a cis woman who chooses to forego reconstructive surgery after breast cancer risks paternalism and dismissal from her doctors. Cis men are sometimes ridiculed for caring too much about their clothing and appearance.

Because caring about one's body is so often seen as ridiculous, when someone *does* claim to care, they are often seen not as sincerely expressing legitimate preferences but as having some underhanded reason. Perhaps, they're a dupe of the patriarchy, or actively advancing some nefarious ideology, or instrumentally pursuing some goal that's not really about their body, or just plain irrational.

Although feminist philosophers have written critically about how various traditions in the Western canon dismiss or devalue the body, these traditions are so ingrained that it's hard for even feminists to avoid falling back into them. We'll briefly outline a few "brainworms" – our word for ideas that lead people to devalue the body – referring the reader to feminist literature that elaborates the relevant points.

4.3.1.1 The "Above All That" Rationality Brainworm

In many cultural settings, caring about the details of physical embodiment is represented as vain, shallow, or petty – as something that decent, rational people don't do. Biology-feels are seen as a distraction from affairs of the mind (or, in some formulations, the spirit), which we are supposed to recognize as what *really* matters. In "liberal" or "progressive" contexts in the United States and peer countries, caring about the body is taken to entail hurtful, bigoted, or reactionary social and political views. In a classic double bind, these values share a social context with ubiquitous pressure to care about and attend to one's body and appearance and are often presented as inseparable from the project of rejecting this pressure. (See Section 4.3.1.3 for more.)

Disdain for the body has a long history. In the Western philosophical tradition, for example, figures from Plato to Aquinas to Kant to Rousseau imagined the ideal person as governed wholly by rationality, separate from the body, unencumbered by "lower" animal functions. This philosophical tendency belongs to a long tradition of presenting women (among others) as undeserving of equal social status because of their supposed intellectual inferiority, which is often entangled with a presumed inability to rationally detach oneself from the mundanely physical (Spelman, 1982; Lloyd, 1984; Gatens, 1991).

When one is told that one is unworthy of equal social standing because one's mind is different, or because one is not sufficiently capable of rational disengagement from the body, one quite sensible response is to point out the flaws of the empirical generalization in question. Accordingly, many prominent feminists, such as Wollstonecraft (1792), Beauvoir (1952), Friedan (1963), and Firestone (1971), have responded to this tendency by insisting that women are no more essentially limited by their physical bodies than men are while leaving intact the assumption that bodies represent a distraction from rationality (Spelman, 1982; Gatens, 1991). The crude version of this that has come down into popular feminist discourse holds that "we're all the same where it matters", in the sense that we can all achieve the same human ideal of rationality, so long as we leave our bodies behind.

If the cause of justice really did require indifference to one's own body, then biology-feels would be dubious on feminist grounds. But we hold, along with feminists like Rich (1976) and Brown (2019), that attention to the affairs of the body, and love and care for one's own body, are not just compatible with feminism but can be understood as integral parts of it. There's nothing irrational about having preferences about one's own body, and these preferences do not by themselves entail anything about one's view of the relative objective merits of other ways of being embodied.

4.3.1.2 The "All About Sex" Brainworm

While caring about one's own body or appearance is often considered shallow, irrational, or even unimaginable, our culture does allow space for caring about *other* people's bodies as objects of sexual interest. In fact, it is often presumed that any interest in one's own body is about its instrumental value as a means of attracting sexual interest from others. So a cis observer, trying to explain a trans person's biology-feels within this interpretive framework, may try to explain them in terms of sexual appetites.

To be clear, there's nothing wrong with having sexual desires or sometimes acting from sexual motives. And many people (cis and trans alike) find that their feels about their own body are entangled with their sexuality. But there is no good reason to assume that all biology-feels can be reduced to sexual desire. The fact that asexual folks can experience biology-feels presents a conspicuous stumbling block for such an account, and, perhaps more saliently, lack of explanatory imagination is not high-quality evidence.

The notion that trans people's biology-feels must stem from sexual motives is not just false, but, given common background assumptions, harmful. When sexual desires stray too far from the realm of procreative heterosexual activity, they are often (problematically) deemed to be pathological, perverted (e.g., Ruddick, 1984; Gray, 1978), or immoral (e.g., Hsiao, 2016). Putting this together with the idea that trans people's biology-feels are really about sex, we get the conclusion that most trans people's biology-feels are pathological or perverted, since they're not directed at anything like traditional heterosexual reproduction. And in fact, there's no shortage of tropes that treat trans people (especially trans women) as sick or perverted simply in virtue of our biology-feels.

In academia, psychologist Ray Blanchard's influential taxonomy explicitly classifies trans women's feels about their own bodies in terms of their ostensible sexual motives. Blanchard (1989) divides trans women into "homosexual transsexuals" (Blanchard's word for trans women who are attracted exclusively to men) and "autogynephilic transsexuals" (Blanchard's word for trans women who are attracted to other women). Both are supposed to be motivated primarily by their sexuality. Very roughly, the story goes that "homosexual transsexuals" want to transition *out of sexual desire for men* while "autogynephilic transsexuals" want to transition because they are men whose heterosexual urges, instead of being directed outward at women, are mistakenly directed inward at *themselves* as women. In other words, Blanchard understands most of trans women's gender feels (including, directly or indirectly, their biology-feels), as motivated by nonnormative sexual desire. There is no room in this account for people to care about their gendered embodiment for any nonsexual reason.[1]

In popular culture, a common transphobic trope is that trans women are men acting out a sexual fetish. Rather than using public spaces for ordinary purposes – bathrooms for eliminating bodily waste, changing rooms for checking the fit of clothing – or wearing women's clothes in an effort to present an intelligible appearance to others – they are, the trope says, doing these things in search of perverse sexual gratification.

The idea that trans women are doing ordinary things for sexual gratification doesn't hold up to serious scrutiny. But it looks more tempting in a society that can't admit that it's okay for people to care about their bodies, not just as a means to sexual gratification, but simply because our bodies are where we spend all of our time.

4.3.1.3 The "Body Positivity" (or "My Body Is Me") Brainworm

Although caring about one's embodiment need not involve any general view of the relative merits of different sorts of bodies, most of us have experienced external pressure to care about our bodies that is packaged with a devaluation of the "wrong" sorts of bodies. This is the source of biology-feels (or something like them) that is most salient in the minds of many cisgender people, and, from this perspective, it is easy to imagine a tension between trans interest in body modification (especially when distilled into a controversial slogan like "born in the wrong body" and feminist values with names like "body positivity" and "body acceptance".

At its best, body positivity promises to be socially transformative. It developed as a facet of fat activism and as a form of resistance against fatphobic social pressure for people, especially women, to diet their bodies into thinness (see Cooper, 2021 for a brief critical overview). The idea that all bodies are worthy of love and acceptance also holds obvious potential for disabled people, trans people, and anyone else whose appearance violates conventional beauty standards.

In transphobic versions of body positivity discourse, however, trans people's biology-feels – in particular, dysphoria and the desire for body modifications – are taken as evidence of inadequate body positivity. If we really loved and accepted our own bodies, why would we want to change them?

But this objection conflates the main insight of body positivity – that we should treat all sorts of bodies as worthy of love and acceptance – with a stronger and harder to defend claim – that individuals must treat all body configurations as equally acceptable *for themselves*. Someone can have strong preferences about their own physical traits, without committing themself to the claim that their preferred physical traits are best for everyone or that there is anything wrong with their dispreferred traits.

Outside the realm of sex and gender, there are many domains where body positivity is easily reconciled with a desire for body modification. Someone with a strong desire to take thyroid medicine, or have a benign cyst removed, is not thereby committed to any negative about others with low thyroxin levels or untreated benign cysts. These particular preferences can be rationalized by appeal to the concept of medical malfunction or abnormality; maybe body positivity is compatible with wanting to fix things that are medically wrong with one's body but not with wanting to modify it in any other way. But other compelling examples cannot be explained away so easily.

A punk who adorns herself with tattoos and piercings is not thereby expressing disdain for others with different aesthetic preferences. Child-free people who seek out tubal ligations or vasectomies are not thereby claiming superiority over parents. Many disabled people find their disabilities neutral or valuable and do not wish to be cured (see Barnes, 2016; Clare, 2017; Johnson, 2003), but their preferences do not amount to the view that able-bodied people are inferior. And none of these preferences or body modifications are readily justified in terms of a traditional view of medical necessity. (Incidentally, all of these preferences are compatible not just with egalitarian views about bodies but also with healthy self-respect and self-love.)

But aren't *some* preferences for body modification likely to be motivated based on general prejudice against types of bodies? What about desires for weight loss or skin lightening? We agree that internalized prejudice is one possible motive for preferences about the shape or appearance of one's body. But it is not the only possible motive. In the case of trans people's biology-feels, it is not the likeliest explanation: people in the dominant society often respond to trans bodies with disgust and horror rather than approval.

4.3.1.4 Can Brainworms Be Cured?

On the view we advocate, there is no a priori right way to have a body. Instead, we envision a world where people choose their own projects for their bodies, based on their individual tastes and capabilities.

Disdain for the body is deeply ingrained in many anglophone cultures, and we're not sure that ridding ourselves of brainworms altogether is a realistic goal. But by cultivating greater awareness of brainworms, we can challenge them when they arise.

4.3.2 The Patriarchy Made You Do It

Our discussion of biology-feels doesn't address objections to behavior-feels that target allegedly problematic features of the behavior in question. Even if there is no a priori right or wrong way to have a body, some people think that certain gendered behaviors are suspicious – so suspicious, in fact, that no rational person could want or enjoy them. (Alleged examples of such behaviors, as we saw in section 3.2.2, include wearing makeup and wearing high heels.) If a gendered behavior is inherently unreasonable or undesirable, then perhaps there are associated behavior-feels that only make sense as the product of some process that is at odds with rationality, such as coercion, brainwashing, or buying into a dubious sexist ideology.

However, this line of reasoning is flawed. While *some* gendered behaviors might be utterly irredeemable, intuition is not a reliable guide as to whether a given behavior has value. As we hope to demonstrate here, the same behavior can hold many meanings, some oppressive, some neutral, and some liberatory. Sexism, lack of imagination, and squeamishness can lead people to dismiss a potentially harmless or liberatory behavior as irredeemable and to dismiss positive feels toward that behavior as a product of patriarchal brainwashing.

4.3.2.1 Personal Practice Is Not a Prescription

In section 3.2.2, we argued that some dismissals of feminine-coded behaviors (like wearing makeup or wearing high heels) are misinterpretations of legitimate critiques of norms that connect those behaviors to the category *woman*. Similar dismissals are often directed at trans women and other transfeminine people who have positive feels toward those behaviors – feels strong enough to motivate them to action even in the face of significant societal punishment. The objection often goes something like this: do you think you have to wear makeup to be a woman?

For many trans women (as for many cis women), the obvious answer is: of course not. Someone who likes to wear makeup isn't thereby endorsing the idea that all women should wear makeup – not even if wearing makeup helps her feel more womanly. Just as someone can drink hot cocoa because it reminds them of home without demanding that everyone drink cocoa when they think of home, or feel powerful while doing sports without thinking that only athletes are powerful, so someone can enjoy the gendered resonances of a behavior without endorsing the idea that all people in their gender category, or only people in their gender category, should engage in the behavior.

4.3.2.2 Design History Is Not Destiny

But what if the patriarchal origins of some behaviors are so unsavory that they contaminate any positive feels we might have about those behaviors? Perhaps it's not just that these behaviors happen to figure in gender norms but that their very nature, and the nature of our feels about them, is deeply shaped by those norms. For example, many skin care products on the market today would not have developed in a society without oppressive and sexist beauty standards. Therefore, (the objection goes), there is something wrong with enjoying those products; it amounts to covertly endorsing the worst aspects of the cosmetic industry.

Most feminists would agree that some behaviors are so deeply shaped by patriarchy that they would not or could not exist without the patriarchy, even if they disagree about which. However, even if a behavior is deeply shaped by the patriarchy, it does not follow that positive feels toward it are misguided, immoral, or a product of brainwashing.

Many of our (not especially gendered) behaviors have also been deeply shaped by exploitative social arrangements but are capable of adapting so that they are independent of, or even resistant to, the arrangements that originally gave rise to them. Medicines developed through unethical animal testing practices are still useful, and while it may be important to pursue reparations for those harmed, there is no point in ceasing to use those medicines and no harm in feeling good about their useful effects. Realistic meat substitutes might not have arisen in a society without widespread factory farming but enjoying them makes no contribution to ongoing factory farming (and in fact, choosing them is one way of decreasing the demand for factory-farmed meat).

Likewise, whether someone engages in a behavior that was originally developed under patriarchal conditions might not have much of an effect on whether those conditions persist. (Women in many fields find that they are targets of sexism irrespective of whether they dress in a stereotypically feminine way.) A behavior that was developed under patriarchal conditions might be usefully deployed for anti-patriarchal purposes, for example, undermining stereotypes. And someone who likes a behavior need not like it because of its unsavory history.

But perhaps some feels are bad, not because the things they're about are shaped by the patriarchy, but because they themselves are shaped by the patriarchy. If they arose under deeply unjust conditions, doesn't that make them inauthentic or at least deeply misguided?

We don't think that desires, preferences, and feels that have been shaped by the patriarchy are automatically misguided. As Wenner (2020) points out, a preference formed under conditions of oppression can nonetheless fit with someone's considered and deeply held values. (These values, after all, were also formed under conditions of oppression.) And as Khader (2020) points out, denying that such preferences are legitimate reinforces oppression by encouraging paternalistic interference and by setting up standards of moral character on which real people – especially people from nondominant groups – are bound to fail. (An ideal trans woman in a just world would prioritize her own well-being and wouldn't care about cissexist standards of "passing". If a real trans woman is put in a situation where her well-being depends on her ability to "pass" by cissexist standards, how can she possibly measure up to such an ideal?)

So we can't judge the adequacy or authenticity of someone's feels based on how a hypothetical version of them would have felt in a just universe. Therefore, pointing out that a gender feel has unsavory patriarchal origins is not enough to establish that it is illegitimate. And to the extent that patriarchy does justify questioning the legitimacy of gender feels, trans people's gender feels are not uniquely or specially blameworthy. Cis people's practice-feels also show the marks of having developed under the patriarchy, whether they are preferences for doing socially necessary but gendered work like child care or orthopedic surgery, or preferences for engaging in practices that are relatively harmless but are associated through patriarchal norms with manhood or womanhood. (Any particular example of a harmless practice can be shot down by a sufficiently suspicious reader, but cis people's preferences concerning appearance, mate choice, and mode of emotional expression somehow seem to come in for less criticism than comparable preferences by trans people.)

4.3.3 What About Category-Feels?

Category-feels, at least as they arise in the trans context, often raise more questions than behavior-feels or biology-feels. After all, gendered behaviors and sexed biology seem to straightforwardly belong to our material reality, so our desires and preferences about them are readily intelligible. But if we set aside the roles that gender categories play in various gender norms, they seem like nothing more than abstract labels without material payoff.

Of course, as things stand now, gender category membership is connected to material payoff through unjust norms. But on our view, gender categories could withstand significant changes to these norms; none of the norms are necessary to the categories' continued existence. And while anyone *could* want anything for bad reasons, trans and nonbinary people's category-feels need not, and typically do not, commit us to endorsing problematic norms.

But why else would anyone care about gender category membership? According to one skeptical outlook, no reasonable person could care, and trans people's claims to care must be attributable to problematic ulterior motives, metaphysical confusion, or both.

This skeptical outlook is typically committed to two claims: first, that trans and nonbinary people who express category-feels must endorse, or at least tacitly accept, traditionalist norms (in the most common variant, category-behavior norms), and second, that our category-feels are just manifestations of our behavior-feels (either desires to engage in behaviors not allowed for our assigned category or desires to avoid behaviors prescribed for our assigned category). Bluntly, it portrays our category-feels as part of a comically ineffective effort to politely ask the patriarchy to exempt us from its rules when our time would be better spent fighting against the rules themselves.

An example of this skeptical outlook is Rebecca Reilly-Cooper's (2016) take on agender folks:

> This desire not to be cis is rational and makes perfect sense, especially if you are female. . . . I, too, would like to be seen as more than just a mother/domestic servant/object of sexual gratification. I, too, would like to be viewed as a human being, a person with a rich and deep inner life of my own, with the potential to be more than what our society currently views as possible for women.
>
> The solution to that, however, is not to call myself agender, to try to slip through the bars of the cage while leaving the rest of the cage intact, and the rest of womankind trapped within it.

Here Reilly-Cooper presents a forced choice: either uphold the category-behavior norms and pursue one's behavioral aspirations by trying to change one's category membership or fight to remove the restrictive category-behavior norms. It is simply unimaginable that someone might be invested in their category membership without accepting the particular norms that Reilly-Cooper objects to. Note, critically, that for Reilly-Cooper's complaint to do the intended work, we must be talking about norms that are publicly recognized and considered generally applicable and binding. An individual's personal feelings about what thinking of themself as a woman means *for them in particular* will not provide the kind of "cage" that makes the concern compelling, unless it is generalized to a view of women in general and unless it attains some kind of wider social currency.

Reilly-Cooper's interpretation of the motives behind category-feels is deeply at odds with trans people's testimony and behavior. Many of us see no conflict between feminist opposition to gender norms and professing strong personal category-feels. Singer–songwriter Laser Malena-Weber, for example, came out as nonbinary less than two years after releasing a song featuring the lyrics "I am a woman and I'm doing it right./I am no matter what I do".[2] While they have clearly revisited the "I am a woman" part of their lyrics, they have shown no sign of repudiating or otherwise backing off from their very public feminist politics.

Both of the authors have personal narratives that illustrate this point. B (B. R. George) knew for years men could wear dresses, and spent time trying to *be* a man in a dress, but ultimately concluded that the "man" part felt like a lie for them. For their part, Ray (R. A. Briggs) has discovered that wearing dresses is more comfortable and more fun now that it doesn't get them perceived as a woman (at least in San Francisco, where a man can wear a dress without being threatened with physical violence). For both of us, our commitment to the notion that people of any category should enjoy the same freedom to choose among behaviors predates any sense of ourselves as trans and nonbinary or any conscious awareness of our own category-feels.

Insofar as people like Reilly-Cooper acknowledge that many trans and nonbinary people profess to reject pernicious gender norms and to have category-feels for other reasons, they tend to paint such category-feels as a form of mysticism – at best akin to respectable theology, and at worst an exercise in metaphysical incoherence. This sort of thinking tends to trade on the background assumption that categories aren't good for anything *except* their role in the network of gender norms that we introduced in Chapter 4. But we'll argue that there are plenty of intelligible reasons for people (whether cis or trans) to care about gender categories that have nothing to do with endorsing gender norms.

This is not to say that trans people are free from internalized sexism. No one, trans or cis, is immune to the psychological effects of a society saturated in pernicious gender norms or blessed with perfect introspective access to the underlying causes of all their feels. But this just means that *any* aspect of human mental life can be shaped by the ubiquitous forces of the sex/gender system. It does not mean that category-feels result directly from any kind of *investment* in pernicious gender norms or that they are more suspect in this regard than any other area of our mental lives.

But on to our positive argument. If category-feels don't require endorsement of category-behavior norms, what's the point having them, and why should anyone care which gender category they belong to?

4.3.3.1 Useful Analogies: Names, Teams, and Marriages

In other domains, it is widely recognized that people care about category membership for reasons that are neither straightforwardly instrumental nor easily attributed to the endorsement of public norms governing the categories. For example, it's considered unsurprising that people care about their names. We don't typically treat this as grounds for suspecting them of insincerity, incompetence, confusion, or moral turpitude. In short, we are inclined to take their feels about names seriously.

When Elizabeth insists on being called "Beth" and not "Liz", we're not shocked. We don't think she owes us an explanation of why she cares, we don't expect her to be narrowly concerned about some instrumental payoff of being called "Beth", and we don't infer that she endorses some public norm or stereotype about which behaviors are normal and appropriate for "Beth"'s as opposed "Liz"'s. Or suppose Mr. Hunter takes it upon himself to change his name and become Mr. Shepherd. The concerned observer who informs him that you don't have to be named "Shepherd" to tend a flock – and urges him to reject a reactionary, stereotypical view of what is possible for people named "Hunter" – is most likely missing the point. If critics protest that either of these people *must* be embracing such stereotypes, because that is the only conceivable reason someone could have a preference among labels, they are not helping their case. In either situation, we are happy to accept that feelings involved are sincere and legitimate, and that the motives behind them may be largely personal in a way that has few or no implications for the general public meaning of the name involved.

This doesn't mean that names are completely detached from all material payoff: they often let us draw fallible inferences about someone's age, ethnicity, class, and gender. People may care about their names for instrumental reasons (wanting a name that's easy to spell or one that will help them land a job); they may associate names with material characteristics (disliking a nickname because it seems babyish or wanting a name that reflects an ethnic heritage). Our point is that even though someone's name doesn't entail any specific set of claims about their material characteristics, we can still make sense of people caring about them for their own sake. Similarly, even though someone's gender category membership doesn't entail any specific set of claims about their sexed biology or about which gendered practices they engage in, category-feels needn't be pointless or even puzzling.

Another analogy comes from augmented reality games like Pokemon Go or Ingress, where players often feel invested in which team they belong to. This is not because they endorse stereotypes associating the teams with certain characteristics: in most ways, the teams are functionally indistinguishable from each other. The relevant material payoffs don't involve any general norm about which sorts of activities are available to which teams but instead constrain which specific other people one can coordinate with (or face off against) in certain multi-participant activities.

A third type of analogy involves subcultural affiliation: the cultural category *goth* participates in plenty of generally recognized aesthetic norms, but these do not fully determine category membership. Goths can listen to non-goth music, and non-goths can listen to goth music. Plenty of imaginable outfits and overall personal aesthetics are compatible with more than one subcultural affiliation. A given look might have specific elements that are more steampunk than goth, more goth than emo, or more emo than metal, but such elements (especially if combined with other elements that cut in another direction) don't necessarily render a look compatible with only a single subcultural affiliation. If both Ada and Blaise wear fishnet arm warmers and stompy boots, listen to the Cure and the Cocteau Twins, and so on, it might still be the case that Ada is goth and Blaise is emo, and that they are both quite invested in their respective affiliations.

Finally, consider a more politically salient example: both major sides of the marriage equality debate in the United States have treated the category *marriage* (associated with words like "marriage", "marry", "wife", "husband", "spouse", "wedding", "divorce", and so on) as important in ways that go beyond narrowly descriptive material payoffs. What else can explain the history of "compromise" proposals that offer another category like *civil union* alongside the promise that it would be a distinct category that enjoyed legal characteristics indistinguishable from those of marriage? Why have marriage equality advocates rejected such proposals, if not for an investment in being placed in the same category as heterosexual married couples? Why have some marriage equality opponents been willing to accept this as a more palatable alternative, if not for an understanding that the category matters over and above its material consequences? There are undoubtedly instrumental reasons to care about whether one's union counts as a marriage, but these are not the only reasons.

So outside of trans politics, it's common for people to care about how they are categorized in ways that cannot be straight-forwardly traced back to norms that give the categories distinct material consequences. We think the aforementioned analogies are common enough to show that category-feels present no distinctive mystery. But there's still something puzzling here: to the extent that membership in gender categories doesn't entail anything about what behaviors one can or should engage in, what positive reasons could someone have for caring about it? The reasons vary from person to person and may be idiosyncratic and opaque, but we want to very briefly sketch some common types of reasons that might be relevant. (The items on our list aren't meant to be exhaustive, definitive, or applicable to any particular cis or trans person's category-feels. Their purpose is just to demystify the idea of category-feels.)

4.3.3.2 Belonging

People care a lot about who they're categorized *with*: someone might want to be on the same Pokemon Go team as their friends or in the same Girl Scout troop as an older sister. Two people might connect at an icebreaker because they share a first name (a friend of B's once said about a new acquaintance, "we bonded over our shared Emily-hood"). Someone might want their union to count as a marriage in order to situate it within a tradition of similar unions. People also care about who they're *not* categorized with. They may change their names to distance themselves from an unpleasant family history or adopt nicknames that distinguish them from similarly named people they dislike.

Distancing needn't be about hatred or contempt; someone might choose to be on a different Pokemon team from a friendly rival or might pick a different nickname from a friend specifically to reduce the risk of confusion in contexts where both are present or narratively salient. Nor is wanting to belong to the same category necessarily a sign of approval. A person might want their own union to count as a marriage in order to transform the institution of marriage, making it less heteronormative and sexist by creating better examples. Or someone might stubbornly keep a name that they coincidentally shared with a famously awful person rather than letting them "ruin" it.

These types of reasons potentially apply as much to gender categories as to other kinds of categories and might come up in any of the ways discussed earlier. For example, a woman (trans or cis) might be invested in her sense of herself as a woman because of her investment in a particular clique or community, or in a more general sense of being "one of the girls", even if she has no particular interest in the behaviors associated with traditional femininity or has an indifferent or ambivalent relationship with stereotypically female biological traits – even if, indeed, she values her particular clique or community of women exactly *because* it rejects the expectations of traditional femininity and cissexism.

4.3.3.3 Continuity

Often, we don't just care about who shares our category membership *now*; we care about continuity over time. Sometimes, we crave connection with the past through shared category membership, like those who want to participate in a tradition of marriage that includes the unions of older relatives, those who value being named after a particular ancestor or an admired historical figure, or those who value connection with a particular religious denomination or sect (even if they don't have much investment in its particular articles of faith, as distinct from those of closely related religious traditions). At other times, we want to deliberately break connections: to specifically not be part of the institution of marriage (even if we have built a life with a long-term partner) or to change our surname specifically because we do not want to share a name with despised ancestors.

We care about continuity within ourselves as well as continuity with others. Someone might want to keep the same name over time for symbolic as well as practical reasons or to adopt a new name that symbolizes a new start in life. We can moreover value a sense of connection with an imagined past that turns out never to have occurred. One might, for example, be invested in an understanding of oneself as named after a legendary figure who was not in fact a historical person. This might be the result of an erroneous understanding of history, but it might also be the result of a self-aware investment in continuity with myth. (One can delight in the image of a symbolic foremother killing a man with a tent peg, without thinking it especially likely that the Biblical Yael was a historical figure.)

Analogous considerations can plausibly apply to gender. One might specifically have a sense of belonging across time with respect to a specific long line of women (or men, or others) in a particular family or close-knit community. Or have a sense of oneself as a woman or a man or something else that is wrapped up in a sense of affiliation with a particular legendary or fictional figure.

4.3.3.4 Personal Resonance

People care about belonging to gender categories not just because it's a way of connecting to others, but because it's a way of connecting to traits: someone might connect being a man to experiencing his body as strong and beautiful or connect being a woman to feeling emotionally attuned with others. This need not amount to endorsing a general social norm to the effect that all men are strong and beautiful or that all women are emotionally attuned with others. There need not even be such a norm; the connection can instead be idiosyncratic and personal.

We can make good philosophical sense of idiosyncratic meanings. Campbell (1997, p. 138), theorizing about the nature of emotions, points out that a feeling can be personal (that is, it can have a meaning that is not determined by shared rules, conventions, norms, and so on) without being inherently private (that is, it need not have a meaning that is unknowable, uninterpretable, or inaccessible to others). There are additional resources, aside from shared norms, that we can use to make sense of each other's feelings, like the causes that occasion those feelings or the behaviors that express those feelings. In the case of category-feels, these resources might include acts of categorization, expressions of happiness or dismay at how we are categorized, requests or demands about how others categorize us, or even the gender categories themselves.

We draw idiosyncratic personal connections about many things besides gender categories. Someone might hate the smell of lavender because it reminds them of their abusive great aunt or love an individual mass-produced trinket that was given to them by a beloved friend (even though it's no different from its assembly line siblings). Someone might encourage a nickname because it was given to them by a childhood friend or avoid a pet name because they associate it with a past lover. We all recognize that these sorts of personal connections can exist separate from norms held in the collective social imagination and that people need not consciously or unconsciously regard them as requiring others to draw similar connections for themselves.

Likewise, gender categories can be personally evocative for someone who wouldn't endorse any corresponding public gender norms and where there is no public norm requiring people to draw the relevant connection. Someone can feel drawn to womanhood because she associates it with her experiences in the Girl Scouts or repelled by womanhood because they had a particularly toxic relationship with the community dynamics at their women's college. Someone can feel drawn to manhood because it makes him think of the camaraderie of his gay men's choir. Trans people's personal connections to gender categories, like cis people's, can be positive or negative: a trans woman's category-feels might be shaped by numerous experiences of manhood "not fitting", but it might also be shaped by fond memories of being "adopted" into a women-centered space, organization, or social group.

The diversity of personal experience being what it is, anything can evoke anything. And for most of us, gender categories have been part of our formative, emotion-laden experiences. So it shouldn't be surprising that people can find gender categories personally evocative in a way that doesn't amount to a political commitment that is binding on everyone or indicate a narrow view about what combinations of gender categories and gendered behaviors are possible.

4.3.3.5 Why Is This So Hard to Believe?

Feels about categories and labels are ubiquitous, and they extend far beyond gender categories. Some have simple, commonplace, relatively straightforward explanations while others are mysterious and difficult to make sense of; perhaps a certain name "just sounds right" in a way that can't easily be traced back to any particular formative influence. All of this is part of the normal, unsurprising flow of the lives of complex, symbol-oriented thinking beings. Why, then, do many people find it hard to believe in the possibility of such category-feels in the context of trans subjectivity?

One obvious consideration is general cissexist and transphobic bias: trans lives and minds are routinely represented as pathological or bizarre – as curiosities in need of explanation – and in that context it is unsurprising that many people have trouble taking trans folks at our word. The equivocations around "gender" and "gender identity" that we saw in Chapters 2 and 3 help enable this skepticism: if "gender identity" already unites category-feels and behavior-feels, then it is natural to understand one as a simple manifestation of the other. And if "gender" names both a system of norms and an inner trait that is supposed to justify and motivate transition, it is easy to leap to the conclusion that the norms must be creating the desire to transition.

Beyond this, there is the very real possibility that not everyone has much in the way of category-feels. Some portion of the population is probably what Ozy Brennan (2015) calls "cis by default" – accepting their cisgender category assignment (and their sexed biology) not because they have any particular positive feels about it, or any negative feels about other categories, but simply because they lack any strong preference. Since people often take themselves to be presumptively normal, someone who is cis by default might have trouble imagining that anyone has strong gender feels about a thing that they themself are indifferent to.

Even when cis people do have category-feels, they may not have cause to notice them. If you are accustomed to being categorized in ways that feel comfortable and appropriate, without any particular effort on your part, you might not realize that you have any particular attachment to the unexamined status quo. Nonetheless, many cis people do seem to have strong preferences regarding gender categorization: they feel intensely awkward if they are misgendered by telemarketers or waitstaff, even when nothing of practical importance hangs on categorization. And cis people expect each other to care about gender categorization: a common response to accidentally misgendering a stranger is to apologize profusely!

4.4 Conclusion

To sum up: some people think that certain sorts of gender feels simply *must* stem from problematic ulterior motives and that having certain sorts of feels for more-or-less non-instrumental reasons is irrational or even impossible. Or at least, they believe this when it comes to trans people's feels.

On the surface of it, it's not clear why this view would be appealing. After all, people have a wide variety of preferences and dispositions that are similar to gender feels, and we are often content to accept them at face value. In this chapter, we have tried to map out some of the reasons behind this selective suspicion of trans people's gender feels and tried to explain why this suspicion is not justified. In fact, it is perfectly possible to have biology-feels, behavior-feels, or category-feels without any kind of especially nefarious or confused motives.

All of this is perfectly compatible with the possibility that some people may experience some gender feels for problematic reasons (which seems hard to deny) – or even that certain types of gender feels are unavoidably problematic. But merely pointing out that they're feels about gendered traits, that they involve the desire to modify one's body, or that they align with traditional femininity does not suffice to show that they're bad – one needs to do the work of presenting specific reasons for suspicion.

There are still some unresolved questions about what categories *are*, which we'll explore in the next chapter.

Notes

1 For a review and critique of Blanchard's typology and related work, see Serano (2010, 2019, 2020a, 2020b, 2021), Ashley (2019a), and the various sources cited therein.
2 The song is "Women Know Math", available at www.youtube.com/watch?v=ClhgnkJ9VQI

References

Ashley, F. (2019a). Science has always been ideological, you just don't see it. *Archives of Sexual Behavior*, *48*(6). https://doi.org/10.1007/s10508-019-01519-7

Ashley, F. (2019b). Thinking an ethics of gender exploration: Against delaying transition for transgender and gender creative youth. *Clinical Child Psychology and Psychiatry*, *24*(2), 223–236. https://doi.org/10.1177/1359104519836462

Ashley, F. (2020). A critical commentary on "rapid-onset gender dysphoria." *The Sociological Review*, *68*(4), 779–799. https://doi.org/10.1177/0038026120934693

Barnes, E. (2016). *The minority body: A theory of disability*. Oxford University Press. https://doi.org/10.1093/acprof:oso/9780198732587.001.0001

Beauvoir, S. D. (1952). *The second sex*. Vintage Books.

Bettcher, T. M. (2009). Trans identities and first-person authority. In L. Shrage (Ed.), *You've changed: Sex reassignment and personal identity* (pp. 98–120). Oxford University Press.

Blanchard, R. (1989). The classification and labeling of nonhomosexual gender dysphorias. *Archives of Sexual Behavior, 18*(4), 315–334. https://doi.org/10.1007/BF01541951

Brennan, O. (2015, January 28). Cis by default. *Thing of Things*. https://thingofthings.wordpress.com/2015/01/28/cis-by-default/

Brown, A. M. (2019). *Pleasure activism: The politics of feeling good*. AK Press.

Campbell, S. (1997). *Interpreting the personal: Expression and the formation of feelings*. Cornell University Press. http://archive.org/details/interpretingpers0000camp

Clare, E. (2017). *Brilliant imperfection: Grappling with cure*. Duke University Press.

Cooper, C. (2021). *Fat activism: A radical social movement* (2nd ed). Intellect Books.

Firestone, S. (1971). *The dialectic of sex* (Rev. ed.). Bantam Books.

Friedan, B. (1963). *The feminine mystique*. W.W. Norton.

Gatens, M. (1991). *Feminism and philosophy: Perspectives on difference and equality*. Indiana University Press.

Gray, R. (1978). Sex and sexual perversion. *Journal of Philosophy, 75*(4), 189–199. https://doi.org/10.2307/2025658

Hsiao, T. (2016). Consenting adults, sex, and natural law theory. *Philosophia, 44*(2), 509–529. https://doi.org/10.1007/s11406-016-9705-z

Johnson, H. M. (2003, February 16). Unspeakable conversations. *The New York Times*. www.nytimes.com/2003/02/16/magazine/unspeakable-conversations.html

Khader, S. J. (2020). The feminist case against relational autonomy. *Journal of Moral Philosophy, 17*(5), 499–526. https://doi.org/10.1163/17455243-20203085

Littman, L. (2018). Parent reports of adolescents and young adults perceived to show signs of a rapid onset of gender dysphoria. *PLoS One, 13*(8), e0202330. https://doi.org/10.1371/journal.pone.0202330

Lloyd, G. (1984). *Man of reason*. University of Minnesota Press.

McGeer, V. (2008). The moral development of first-person authority. *European Journal of Philosophy, 16*(1), 81–108. https://doi.org/10.1111/ejop.2008.16.issue-1

Moran, R. (2001). *Authority and estrangement: An essay on self-knowledge*. Princeton University Press.

Narayan, S. K., Hontscharuk, R., Danker, S., Guerriero, J., Carter, A., Blasdel, G., Bluebond-Langner, R., Ettner, R., Radix, A., Schechter, L., & Berli, J. U. (2021). Guiding the conversation – types of regret after gender-affirming surgery and their associated etiologies. *Annals of Translational Medicine, 9*(7), 605. https://doi.org/10.21037/atm-20-6204

Raymond, J. (1994). *The transsexual empire: The making of the she-male* (2nd ed.). Teachers College Press.

Reilly-Cooper, R. (2016, June 28). Gender is not a spectrum. *Aeon.* https://aeon.co/essays/the-idea-that-gender-is-a-spectrum-is-a-new-gender-prison

Restar, A. J. (2020). Methodological critique of Littman's (2018) parental-respondents accounts of "rapid-onset gender dysphoria." *Archives of Sexual Behavior, 49*(1), 61–66. https://doi.org/10.1007/s10508-019-1453-2

Rich, A. C. (1976). *Of woman born: Motherhood as experience and institution* (1st ed.). W.W. Norton.

Riddell, C. (1980). Divided sisterhood a critical review of Janice Raymond's the trans-sexual empire. *News From Nowhere.*

Ruddick, S. (1984). Better sex. In R. Baker & F. Elliston (Eds.), *Philosophy and sex.* Prometheus Books.

Schilt, K., & Westbrook, L. (2015). Bathroom battlegrounds and penis panics. *Contexts, 14*(3), 26–31. https://doi.org/10.1177/1536504215596943

Serano, J. (2010). The case against autogynephilia. *International Journal of Transgenderism, 12*(3), 176–187. https://doi.org/10.1080/15532739.2010.514223

Serano, J. (2020a). Autogynephilia, ad hoc hypotheses, and handwaving. *Medium.* https://juliaserano.medium.com/autogynephilia-ad-hoc-hypotheses-and-handwaving-cecca4f6563d

Serano, J. (2020b). Autogynephilia: A scientific review, feminist analysis, and alternative 'embodiment fantasies' model. *The Sociological Review, 68*(4), 763–778. https://doi.org/10.1177/0038026120934690

Serano, J. (2021). Autogynephilia and anti-trans activism. *Medium.* https://juliaserano.medium.com/autogynephilia-and-anti-trans-activism-23c0c6ad7e9d

Spelman, E. V. (1982). Woman as body: Ancient and contemporary views. *Feminist Studies, 8*(1), 109–131.

Stone, S. (1992). The empire strikes back: A posttranssexual manifesto. *Camera Obscura: Feminism, Culture, and Media Studies, 10*(2), 150–176. https://doi.org/10.1215/02705346-10-2_29-150

Veale, J. F., Peter, T., Travers, R., & Saewyc, E. M. (2017). Enacted stigma, mental health, and protective factors among transgender youth in Canada. *Transgender Health, 2*(1), 207–216. https://doi.org/10.1089/trgh.2017.0031

Wenner, D. M. (2020). Nodomination and the limits of relational autonomy. *International Journal of Feminist Approaches to Bioethics, 13*(2), 28–48. https://doi.org/10.3138/ijfab.13.2.2020-01-08

Wiepjes, C. M., Nota, N. M., Wensing-Kruger, S. A., de Jongh, R. T., Bouman, M.-B., Steensma, T. D., Cohen-Kettenis, P., Gooren, L. J. G., & Kreukels, B. P. C. (2018). The Amsterdam cohort of gender dysphoria study (1972e2015): Trends in prevalence, treatment, and regrets. *The Journal of Sexual Medicine, 15*, 582–590.

Wilson, E. C., Chen, Y.-H., Arayasirikul, S., Raymond, H. F., & McFarland, W. (2016). The impact of discrimination on the mental health of trans*female youth and the protective effect of parental support. *AIDS and Behavior, 20*(10), 2203–2211. https://doi.org/10.1007/s10461-016-1409-7

Wollstonecraft, M. (1792). *A vindication of the rights of woman with strictures on political and moral subjects.* Joseph Johnson.

5

OUR PRINCESS IS IN ANOTHER CASTLE

There Is No Essence of Womanhood

5.1 Against Reduction

The main goal of this text has been to develop conceptual tools to clarify conversations around gender, including a distinction between gender categories on the one hand and various biological and behavioral traits on the other. This distinction played an important role in Chapter 2, where we distinguished category-feels from biology-feels and from behavior-feels, and in Chapter 3, where we distinguished norms about categories from norms entirely concerned with biology, behavior, or both. In Chapter 4, we did some additional work to argue that the category-feels we introduced in Chapter 2 should be taken seriously. But up to this point, we have tried to remain noncommittal about the ontological status of gender categories, and what we've said is compatible with a wide variety of approaches.

Still, what we have done so far raises some obvious questions about what gender categories are. In this chapter, we propose an approach that treats gender categories as full-fledged distinct items in our ontology, alongside biology and behavior. (In other words, gender categories are *irreducible*.) We will motivate this approach, fill in some details to show how it might work, and defend it against accusations of circularity and mysticism.

Philosophers sometimes assume that the ontology of gender categories is *the* key issue in trans politics, and that what we

DOI: 10.4324/9781003053330-5

need to vindicate trans people's self-understanding is a comprehensive theory of categories like *woman*, *man*, and (sometimes) *genderqueer* or *nonbinary*. That's not how we see things. The work we've done in previous chapters largely stands or falls independently of our theory about the nature of gender categories. And most of the ideas we'll introduce in this chapter, such as the value of gender self-determination and the idea that gender categories need not be reducible to something else in order to be coherent, are defensible independently of the details of our particular approach. This chapter provides one example of a trans-friendly ontology of gender categories but not the only possible one.

The main motivation for our approach is political: we believe in a principle of self-determination with respect to gender categories, which says (roughly) that we should classify people into gender categories according to their sincerely expressed wishes and not according to our own prejudices or projections. Our commitment to self-determination does not reflect the "common sense" of the dominant society, and it is not intended to. Rather, it reflects an alternative to the mainstream status quo – one that has already been taken up in many queer and trans-inclusive subcultural spaces, that could be taken up more widely and that we take to be a normative commitment of some important traditions in queer and trans politics.

But gender self-determination is possible only if gender categories are irreducible. To see why, recall our characters Ada, Blaise, and Cass from Section 2.2.4. These characters are alike in their sexed biological characteristics (all three have a 46,XX karyotype, and various sexed bodily features stereotypically associated with that karyotype), in their gendered behavior (all three sport crew cuts and lift weights), and in their feels about each of these things, but they differ in their category-feels (with Ada preferring to be classified as a woman and not a man, Blaise as a man and not a woman, and Cass as a nonbinary person who is neither a woman nor a man).

We first introduced this example to illustrate how category-feels can come apart from biology-feels and behavior-feels, but it also highlights the appeal of treating gender categories as if they exist over and above sexed biology and gendered behavior. For not only do Ada, Blaise, and Cass *identify* with different gender categories (in the sense of having and avowing different feels about them), our self-determination principle tells us that, since they declare themselves to have different category-feels, we have excellent reason to *recognize them as belonging* to different gender categories. We should say that Ada is a (cisgender) woman, Blaise is a (transgender) man, and Cass is a nonbinary person.

If Ada is a woman, Blaise is a man, and Cass is nonbinary, it would seem that gender categories cannot reduce to sexed biology, gendered behavior, biology-feels, behavior-feels, norms connecting biological behavioral traits, or any combination of these. (After all, Ada, Blaise, and Cass are situated alike with respect to all these other properties, but they still differ in how we should categorize them.) Thus, if we accept self-determination with respect to gender categories, we find ourselves in a position where it is difficult to avoid recognizing gender categories as full-fledged elements of our ontology and not reducible to the other components of the gender system.

Opponents of gender self-determination often notice that it entails a version of irreducibility and argue that this makes gender self-determination viciously circular. In popular discourse, self-determination for the "woman" category is often stated as something like the following:[1]

SELF-ID:[2] A person is a woman if and only if they *identify as a woman*.

But then, the objection goes, concept of *identifying as a woman* either appeals to an antecedent understanding of *woman* (in which case, treating it as a criterion of womanhood is viciously circular), or else it is primitive (in which case, it is troublingly mysterious, magical, and unverifiable), or else it amounts to believing that certain stereotypes of womanhood apply to oneself (in which case it is objectionable on political grounds).[3] In the wider discourse, this style of objection is often presented as some version of the question "Well then how do you define 'woman'?"

SELF-ID may be in need of revision and clarification, but even in its current form, it's perfectly coherent. Worries about vicious circularity disappear if we understand SELF-ID not as a definition of the term "woman", or as an analysis of the concept of womanhood but as a proposal about how we should gender people (that is, as a sort of "admissions policy" for a gender category). It describes a (proposed) state of affairs in which category membership is available on an opt-in basis.

To see how this could work, let's revisit the analogy with personal names from Section 4.3.3.1. We contend that SELF-ID is no more incoherent than the analogous policy for names:

SELF-NAMING: A person is named "Emily" if and only if they claim the name "Emily" for themself.

SELF-NAMING does not accord perfectly with the prevailing social reality: most societies have some more involved procedural requirements for changing one's legal or official name. But for many purposes it's not that far off: the name (or nickname or professional name) that someone goes by in many parts of ordinary life is a matter of self-determination. And self-determination for names is typically a good policy: if someone tells you what name they do or do not answer to, it is usually appropriate to respect their wishes in this matter.[4]

The reason that SELF-NAMING is not troubling (and is not vulnerable to incoherence- and stereotype-based objections) is that it is not a definition of what it is to be named "Emily" but a proposed admissions policy for being named "Emily". A name like "Emily" is out there in our social reality, maintained by our collective awareness that such a name exists, but the property of being named "Emily" is not reducible to any set of name-independent traits. We wouldn't expect a nontrivial definition of being named "Emily".[5] Moreover, even if people don't currently follow a policy of name self-determination, this tells us nothing about whether or not they could. The policies and customs that govern our naming practices can be revised.

There are various possible ways of developing a fleshed-out, philosophical theory of names. But regardless of how the details work, naming self-determination is clearly a possibility. What goes for names goes for gender categories: just as SELF-NAMING could function as an admissions policy for the (undefined and irreducible) property of being named "Emily", so something like SELF-ID could function as an admissions policy for the (undefined and irreducible) property of being a woman.

This provides a(n admittedly rough) picture how it is possible for gender categories to function as full-fledged objects, and of how gender self-determination is likewise possible. It doesn't show that gender self-determination is desirable, and a systematic exploration of that question is beyond the scope of this book. But it does give us reason to think that communities that observe gender self-determination are doing something prima facie coherent, which could in principle be generalized to the wider society.

It is our hope that many readers will find the analogy with naming adequate – that they will be content to accept that gender self-determination and irreducible gender categories are likewise coherent. In the remainder of this chapter, we flesh out some of our thoughts on the concept of gender self-determination, the use of gendered language, and the ontology of gender categories. Much of this can be seen as an exercise in theoretical bookkeeping, and from time to time we will often adopt one approach – or express ambivalence as to our preferred approach – when alternative theoretical approaches could deliver largely the same "big picture" payoff for self-determination. Depending on their preferred theoretical approach and their perspective on the naming case, the reader may from time to time find that they prefer a formally distinct approach in a similar spirit, but we hope that the reader will be able to "fill in" analogous details and convince themself that the foundational issues raised by gender self-determination are not uniquely troubling or even especially distinctive.

The plan of the rest of the chapter, then, is as follows. In Section 5.2, we take a closer look at the idea of gender self-determination, at different ways of formulating it, and at various caveats and qualifications. In Section 5.3, we turn to the question of how we should wield gendered language in the here-and-now, and in Section 5.4, we introduce some moving parts that can be used to connect our views about the use of gender category terms to a more precise semantic theory. We then turn to the ontology of gender categories, defending gender self-determination, and the irreducibility it introduces, against charges of incoherence in Section 5.5. Sections 5.6–5.8 develop a trans-friendly ontology of gender categories (which is not the only possible ontology but one way of developing a metaphysical theory that makes room for self-determination).

5.2 Gender Self-Determination

Gender self-determination goes by various names, and receives various justifications, in the queer and trans literature. Its advocates usually believe that it should extend beyond category membership to how one configures one's body and participates in gendered social practices. We agree, but for the purposes of this chapter, we're interested primarily in the idea that gender *categorization* should be self-determined. We draw inspiration from Bettcher (2009) and Bornstein (1994), among others.

Bettcher (2009) argues that people have a kind of ethical "first-person authority" with respect to gender categorization and likens it to the authority that people have to report what they are thinking and feeling. Just as it's wrong to tell someone what they *really* feel, rather than taking their word on the matter, so it's wrong to tell someone what gender category they *really* belong to. This is not because people are infallible about their mental states or their gender category membership but because assuming the authority to make declarations about someone else's mental states or gender category membership is an infringement on their autonomy – people have a right to decide for themselves.

Bornstein (1994, p. 123) frames gender self-determination as "consensual gender", punning on the phrase "consensual sex".[6] She contrasts consensual gender with coercive practices that are still lamentably common:

> We're born: a doctor assigns us a gender. It's documented by the state, enforced by the legal profession, sanctified by the church, and it's bought and sold in the media. We have no say in our gender – we're not allowed to question it, play with it, work it out with our friends, lovers, or family.

Consensual gender, on the other hand, "is respecting each other's definitions of gender", "doesn't force its way in on anyone", and "welcomes all people as gender outcasts – whoever is willing to admit to it" (Bornstein, 1994, p. 124). Similar ideas appear in (Serano, 2007, p. 166), and (Feinberg, 1998, p. 1), are widespread in various trans liberation and social justice movements, and are implicit in the "best practices" recognized by many queer and otherwise trans-inclusive communities.

We agree with Bettcher and Bornstein about the following central points: first, the current practices of the dominant culture don't give people much of a say about how they're sorted into gender categories. Second, these practices are bad; they prevent people from living autonomous, happy, and authentic lives. And third, we could adopt better practices without thereby eliminating gender categories from our social world.

What might better practices look like? Activists tend to agree that in a better world, someone's avowal of category membership

(e.g., asserting "I am a man") or nonmembership (e.g., asserting "I am not a man") would not be diminished, invalidated,
or called into question by their appearance, their medical circumstances, or their feels regarding these.[7] Representative activist and community writings on this theme include Jones (2013),
Taylor (2013), Finch (2015). In our experience, many subcultural spaces *already* operate in this way.

It is important for what follows that self-determination provides a *sufficient* condition for attributing category membership
or nonmembership but the question of whether any kind of
avowal should be a *necessary* condition is more fraught. Should
we wait to call someone a boy, a girl, or nonbinary until they
have made a declaration? This would require significant changes
to our child-rearing practices (see Gould (1978) for lighthearted
fiction about what these changes might look like, Green and
Friedman (2013) for real-life stories of parents trying to put
them into practice, and Brantz (2017) and Labelle (2018a, 2018b,
2018c, 2018d, 2018e, 2018f, 2018g) for representative activist
and community writing on these themes). Barnes (2022) argues
that making avowals necessary for ascribing membership would
have harmful consequences for cognitively disabled women and
girls.[8] And it seems implausible that explicit avowal should be
required for attributing nonmembership: there are probably
some non-men who have never explicitly disclaimed manhood
because the possibility has never arisen.[9] So while we assume that
an ideal of gender self-determination requires us to treat sincere
avowals as sufficient grounds for ascribing category membership,
we'll withhold judgment on whether such avowals are necessary.

Versions of gender self-determination are often articulated in
terms of *identifying as* a member of a particular gender category.
Using the framework from Chapter 2, we might understand "identifying as" either in terms of having certain category-feels or in
terms of communicative acts like avowals of category membership.
The difference between these is important in theory, but the practical gap between them is not large. Sincere avowals of category

membership typically reflect corresponding category-feels, and such avowals are an indispensable source of evidence about others' category-feels, so whichever of these we endorse in principle, we will end up making similar attributions of category membership in practice.[10] Here, we mostly focus on explicit avowals.

If we focus on avowals, we need to rule out the usual exceptions. For example, gender self-determination does not require us to take avowals seriously when they are made in jest or under duress. So (among other things) we are concerned only with deliberate, voluntary, sincere avowals. We could then entertain various notions of sincerity: for purposes of self-determination, is a sincere avowal one that accurately reflects category-feels, or one that reflects an intention to claim membership (or nonmembership) in a category,[11] or is either of these sufficient, or are both necessary, or is the correct choice of sincerity condition context-sensitive? Nothing we do here requires us to commit to a particular answer to this question, so we leave it open.

The conversations we're engaging with typically focus on *woman* and *man* categories (with varying degrees of recognition of nonbinary alternatives) in the context of a distinctly nonrepresentative sample of world cultures. While we think that gender self-determination works well in these cases, we are reluctant to say that it should apply to absolutely all gender categories. If culturally specific categories like *hijra*, *burrnesha*, *fa'atama*, and *fa'afafine* count as gender categories in our sense, a reasonable principle of gender self-determination should not make them available to someone with no particular connection to the associated cultural sphere. Similarly, if *intersex* is a gender category (one with a great deal of overlap with such categories as *woman* and *man*), then we don't want to say that mere self-identification should be treated as sufficient grounds for being recognized as a member of it. We do, however, take self-determination to apply to the following:

- The *woman* and *man* categories.
- A general-purpose *nonbinary* category.[12]

- Gender classifications understood in terms of one's relationship (or lack thereof) to other categories, such as *genderfluid*, *bigender*, *agender*, *demigirl*, and *demiboy*, in cases where these involve claiming membership (or partial, intermittent, ambivalent or quasi- membership) only in categories to which gender self-determination applies.
- Ad hoc self-descriptive labels: if Cass declares that their gender category is *cactus* (see section 5.9), then we should designate them accordingly.

Philosophers writing about gender categorization often focus on questions about who *in fact* is a woman, a man, nonbinary, and so on. We, on the other hand, understand gender self-determination primarily as a claim about who we should *recognize as* a woman, a man, nonbinary, and so on. But isn't the best way of deciding how to categorize people just determining what they really are? Following Kukla and Lance (2022), Dembroff (2017), and Payton (2022), we think not. In the next section, we say more about why.

5.3 Gender Ascriptions

If we are fortunate enough to find ourselves in a social context where gender self-determination is already standard practice, then the people we ought to recognize as women, men, etc. already *are* recognized as women, men, etc. by the community. But what if we find ourselves in one of the many spaces where gender self-determination is still a fringe position? For example, suppose that Blaise is not generally recognized as a man, even though he ought to be. In this scenario, should we be willing to assert "Blaise is a man"? And is Blaise really a man? To address these questions, we'll need to consider the various things we might be *doing* by saying "Blaise is a man".

First, we might be *describing* some social fact about Blaise and manhood. There are many kinds of descriptive content that could be involved, but one obvious (though contentious) candidate analysis is that we are reporting that the community in fact recognizes Blaise as a man. (One way of understanding Haslanger's (2012) account would imply something like this.)[13] On this sort of account "Blaise is a man" would simply be false in a social context where most people do not recognize Blaise as a man.

Second, we might want to *shape* the social facts. Whether Blaise is recognized as a man is in large part *constituted by*, or at least a *direct product of*, people's saying (or declining to say) things like "Blaise is a man" (or using "he" pronouns for Blaise, or referring to Blaise as someone's brother or son or uncle or boy-friend). In our capacity as members of the community, when we speak of Blaise as a man, we are more or less unavoidably con-tributing to the social facts of whether (and to what extent) the community recognizes Blaise as one.[14] So when we say "Blaise is a man" we are, in a sense, casting our vote in favor of the com-munity recognizing Blaise as a man.[15]

Third, we might want to *communicate a value judgment* about the social facts. Suppose that Ada (who endorses gender self-determination) and Diana (who does not) have a dispute: Ada says, "Blaise is a man" and Diana says, "no, she's a woman". Beyond making opposing contributions to the community's gendering processes, Ada and Diana are communicating a disa-greement about what those practices *ought* to be: Ada thinks the community *ought to* recognize Blaise as a man, and Diana thinks it *ought not* to.[16]

Recognizing that gendered language can be used not just to describe the "facts on the ground" but also to shape those facts and to express value judgments about them helps us to make sense of these sorts of debates about trans inclusion and gender ascriptions. When Diana says "Blaise is a woman" and Ada retorts "No, he's a man", they need not disagree about Blaise's medi-cal history, the current state of prevailing gendering practices in the wider society, or the degree to which other people and institutions currently recognize Blaise as a man or a woman.[17] For all transphobes' talk about the importance of "biological reality", these disputes are not really about biology and need not involve disagreement about the predicted outcome of any biomedical *experimentum crucis*. Instead, they involve disagreement about how Blaise (and people like him) ought to be gendered and a battle to control the facts of how he is gendered.[18]

We are often doing more than one of these things when we say, "Blaise is a man", and, at least in principle, it might turn out that the different functions of language are at cross-purposes. Suppose, for example, that the community is virtually unanimous in its refusal to recognize Blaise as a man, but that we think Blaise ought to be recognized as a man, and would like to do our part to bring about such recognition. Should we await a settled account of the descriptive content of "Blaise is a man" to assure us that this sentence is true, or should we go ahead and say it, on the grounds that it makes an appropriate contribution to gender recognition?

We think that, in general, our primary obligation is to use language that enacts whatever gendering arrangements justice requires.[19] This means that sometimes, it is right to assert that Blaise is a man even when this doesn't reflect the community's prevailing gendering practices. That is, we think that ethics comes first and that matters of descriptive truth or falsehood cannot absolve us of responsibility for the social facts that we create with our words. On this point, we take ourselves to be in broad agreement with Kukla and Lance (2022) and Dembroff (2017).

But is it true that Blaise is a man? In general, how should we understand the truth conditions of gender ascriptions? Kukla and Lance (2022) are noncommittal about truth conditions on the grounds that they are simply not the important consideration here. We're inclined to adopt Kukla and Lance's approach, since we are more concerned with what this language does and how it ought to be used than we are with the question of truth, but we want to emphasize that our account is compatible with a range of views about the truth conditions of gender ascriptions, including two examples we discuss here.

Dembroff (2017) holds that "woman" and "man" pick out roughly the people already recognized as women and men, even in settings where these practices are unjust. On Dembroff's analysis, justice would sometimes compel us to say things that are technically false, as a way of shaping a better world.

Diaz-Leon (2016), on the other hand, holds that "woman" and "man" pick out roughly the people who *ought* to be recognized as women and men, respectively, whether or not they are actually recognized as such. On Diaz-Leon's analysis, what justice compels us to say about Blaise being a man, Cass not being a woman, and so on is true because the standards of justice are built into the semantics of terms like "woman" and "man".

Analyses in the style of Dembroff (2017) and Kukla and Lance (2022) emphasize the role of terms like "woman" and "man" in shaping the social reality of who is recognized as belonging to which category while analyses in the style of Diaz-Leon (2016) focus more on the role of these terms in expressing value judgments about this social reality. But it turns out that these different approaches get us to about the same place for practical purposes: when Blaise is not recognized as a man, but ought to be, Dembroff and Diaz-Leon disagree as to whether sentences like "Blaise is a man" are true or false, but they agree that we ought to assent to such sentences.

In the next section, we'll precisify some of the ideas from this section. (This is also the point in the chapter at which we will start paying closer attention to the sorts of fiddly technical distinctions beloved of analytic philosophers but which might try the patience of other readers.)

5.4 From Gender Categories to Gendered Terms

We've noted that gender self-determination is compatible with a variety of claims about the truth conditions of sentences like

"Blaise is a man", and we've pointed the reader toward two accounts that disagree on this issue but are consistent with gender self-determination. For present purposes, we don't think it's necessary to choose from among the available approaches. But we want to introduce some conceptual distinctions, which will help us to frame the choice points in disputes about the semantics of words like "woman" and "man" and to formulate our claims in the rest of the chapter. So let's distinguish three types of things that are frequently conflated.

First, there are the gender categories themselves. We *don't* think that categories like *woman*, *man*, and *nonbinary* are best understood in terms of properties shared among all their members; that picture is at odds with gender self-determination. Rather, gender categories exist because, like our stock of available names, they belong to our shared social imagination. In order to distance gender categories from words like "woman" and "man", we'll refer to them with schematic uppercase letters: the category associated with women and girls will be F, and the category associated with men and boys will be M. (We'll have more to say about the nature of gender categories in Sections 5.6–5.9, but for now, all we need to posit is their independent existence.)

Next, there are relations that hold between people and gender categories, and given a relation and a gender category G, there is a property of standing in that relation to G. So, for instance, we have the property of *being gendered as a G* in a given social context. (This property is about social recognition: if the people around Ada are inclined to recognize her as a woman, a sister, someone to be addressed as "ma'am", etc., then Ada is gendered as an F.) We won't assume that *being gendered as a G* is the same as actually *being a G*. For any gender category G, there is also the property of *being gendered as not a G*. (So if the people around Ada withhold ascriptions of womanhood, act uncomfortable or confused when she walks into the women's bathroom, etc., then she is gendered as not an F.) Category-feels involve various more complex relations between people and gender categories, including the conviction that one is a G, the desire to be gendered as a G, and other attitudes about one's being (gendered as) a G or as not a G.

Finally, there are *words*[20] associated with these gender categories: for example, in English, "woman", "girl", "lady", "grrrl", "she", "mother", "sister", "aunt", "girlfriend", "empress" etc., are all words understood as (mainly, but perhaps not exclusively) *for Fs*, while "man", "boy", "he", "Mr.", "son", "brother", "nephew", "husband", "fuckboy", "himbo", etc. are all words understood as (mainly, but perhaps not exclusively) *for Ms*.[21]

Having distinguished these pieces of the puzzle, we can recognize a variety of possible perspectives on what exactly they have to do with each other. For our purposes, the central question is, what do the meanings of words like "woman" and "man" (and the truth conditions of sentences like "Ada is a woman" and "Ada is a man") have to do with categories like F and M?

We might say that the relation of *being gendered as* does (almost) all the work, so that, at least for truth-conditional purposes, "woman" is equivalent to "person who is gendered as an F" and "man" is equivalent to "person who is gendered as an M" (or "adult who is gendered as an M"). The views developed by Haslanger (2012) and Dembroff (2017) arguably do something like this, so that the question of who is gendered as an M largely settles the question of who we can truthfully call a "man" (but perhaps not the question of who we *should* call a "man").

Another option puts more conceptual distance between properties like *being gendered as an F* or as an M and the semantics of words like "woman" and "man". A simple account along these lines might treat "man" as equivalent to "adult who ought to be gendered as an M", but more complex variations are possible.[22] This latter sort of approach allows "Blaise is a man" to be true in a social context where Blaise is not gendered as an M. We can understand Diaz-Leon (2016) as taking this approach.

So far, we haven't said much about properties like *being an F* and *being an M*. Given the setup as we've described it, we might have a three-way conceptual distinction between the sorts of questions exemplified by (1), (2), and (3):

(1) Who *is gendered as an M?*
(2) Who really *is an M?*
(3) Who can truthfully be called a "man"?

Many authors simply do not treat (2) and (3) as interestingly distinct, and so far, we've been concerned mostly with the relationship between questions like (1) and questions like (3). But how do questions like (2) fit in?

We could simply do away with the notion of really *being an F*, *being an M*, or *being a G* for any other gender category G. Here, we sketched two different approaches to understanding words like "woman" and "man" in terms of being *gendered as an F* and being *gendered as an M*, without reference to the *(really) is* relation, and we might take this as a sign that the *(really) is* relation is theoretically superfluous and perhaps that questions like (2) are meaningless. What we have to say in this chapter is largely compatible with this approach, but we don't want to commit ourselves to it.

Alternatively, we could place more emphasis on the distinction between questions like (2) and questions like (3). Following Payton (2022), we might distinguish between the extensions of our gender terms (which are constrained by semantic and conceptual commitments) and the properties that explain gendered phenomena (which must answer to social reality). This view allows for the possibility that Blaise is an *M*, but the sentence "Blaise is a man" is false because the English word "man" fails to pick out all and only the people who *really are Ms*.

The picture that emerges is one with two important choice points: the first concerned with the relationship between the properties of *being gendered as a G* and really *being a G*, and the second concerned with the relationship between the property of really *being a G* and the semantics of various words associated with Gs. (Most of the time, we are interested in the relationship between *being gendered as a G* and the semantics of G-associated words, which could in principle represent a distinct choice point but which we won't discuss independently beyond what we've already said.)

If we want to adopt this three-way distinction, a loosely Dembroff-style approach would say that *being gendered as a G* and really *being a G* are equivalent and that the semantics of G-associated words is to be understood in terms of the property of really *being a G* and that in particular we can only truthfully call someone a "man" or a "boy" if he really *is an M*. On this approach, the relationship between the property of really *being a G* and the semantics of G-associated words may still be quite complex because there are significant additional qualifications (as in the case of "empress") or because connection is fuzzier and more tolerant of exceptional cases where a term accurately applies to people outside of the category that the term is "for" (as might be the case with "himbo", "fuckboy", and at least some personal pronouns).

On a loosely Diaz-Leon-style approach, two distinct options present themselves. One option is to make use of the distinction between really *being a G* and *being gendered as a G*, so that for example, Blaise really *is an M* if and only if he ought to *be gendered as an M*. We could then understand the semantics of various G-associated words in exactly the same way as the Dembroff-style approach we just sketched. (We think this option is a more intuitive and natural way of fleshing out the main idea of Diaz-Leon's (2016) proposal within the present framework.) Another option is to agree with the Dembroff-style approach that really *being a G* is equivalent to *being gendered as a G* and to complicate the relationship between *being a G* and the associated vocabulary. We could say that this vocabulary is not for those who are in fact Gs but rather for those who ought to be Gs, so that, for example, "man" truthfully applies to those adults for whom it ought to be the case that they *are Ms*.

Taking a step back: we have distinguished between gender categories like F and M, properties like *being gendered as an F* and perhaps *being an M*, and gendered words like "woman" and "man". Drawing these distinctions has helped us situate a range of existing approaches to the truth conditions of sentences like "Blaise is a man". Another advantage of these distinctions is that they enable us to characterize the meaning of words like "man" in terms of who is or ought to be *gendered as an M* without formal circularity.

Offering noncircular characterizations of these views is helpful because, as we mentioned in Section 5.1, accusations of vicious circularity and closely connected accusations of meaninglessness are sometimes leveled against gender self-determination. We take up these accusations explicitly in the next section. (Readers who are already inclined to dismiss them are welcome to skip to Section 5.6, where we begin to develop a positive ontology of gender categories.)

5.5 Meaninglessness Objections

We find the idea of gender self-determination ethically and politically compelling: it is a valuable norm in those spaces where it currently prevails, and it ought to be adopted by the wider society. For the purposes of this book, we'll assume that its value is evident, and we won't consider political or ethical objections against it.

But many trans-antagonistic voices have gone beyond claiming that gender self-determination is politically unpalatable (we of course disagree) or that it does not accord with current mainstream practice (this is demonstrably true): they have argued that it is in principle incoherent, mystical, circular, or otherwise ruled out on logical, conceptual, or metaphysical grounds. Gender self-determination, according to the objectors, would render gender categories (or category-terms) meaningless.

What does "meaningless" mean? We'll briefly consider a few versions of the objection that are implicitly addressed by what we've already said, before turning to some novel (though still unsuccessful) versions in Sections 5.5.1–5.5.3.

There are many ways of interpreting the "meaninglessness" objection. One possible objection claims that under a regime of gender self-determination, categorizing someone as "nonbinary", "woman", and "man" would not entail anything about their gendered behaviors or sexed biology. But advocates of gender self-determination shouldn't see this as a problem. In fact, it's the whole point: the legitimacy of someone's self-description as a woman, a man, nonbinary, etc. shouldn't depend on their participating in womanly, manly, or androgynous behaviors (we take this to be a commitment of many strands of feminist thought) or possessing any particular sexed biology (we take this to be a requirement for any meaningful program of trans inclusion).

A second possible objection claims that under a regime of gender self-determination, gender categories would be unimportant, and no one could have a legitimate stake in how they were gendered. But this doesn't follow from the observation that gender categories would be irreducible. Recall our discussion of personal names in Chapter 4: although many personal names have little-to-no descriptive payoff, people often care about their names, and we understand that they have reasons to care. Calling someone by their preferred name is generally deemed to be a requirement of basic norms of civility and respect. Thus, the kind of meaninglessness that is required by gender self-determination does not entail that something is "meaningless" in a trivializing or pejorative sense. (The reader is referred to Chapter 4 for more details.)

A third claims that a principle of gender self-determination would deprive us of the necessary vocabulary to talk about important material realities of experiences of privilege and oppression under patriarchy, of sexed biology, and so on. But this worry is implausible: even if we stopped using gender category terms altogether, there is a wide range of precise terms that can be used to single out specific phenomena. One of the projects of Chapters 2 and 3 was to develop an alternative vocabulary for talking about various aspects of gendered embodiment. The reader is referred to Briggs and George (2019) for some discussion on the kinds of vocabulary that trans-inclusive communities often use to meet these various needs, and to Freeman and López (2018) for discussion on how biomedical terminology without reference to gender categories might work.

A fourth claims that if we make room for gender self-determination, then gender categories will fail to pick out any genuine property: there is nothing substantive that all women (or all men, or all nonbinary people) have in common – not anatomy, not social proclivities, not interests, and not any form of shared oppression. If the feminist project is meant to unite women against shared oppression, then women must have some property in common (Haslanger (2012) calls this the "commonality problem"), and so gender self-determination is a threat. We point the reader toward the literature explaining how feminism can succeed as a project even if there is nothing women have in common, including Spelman (1988), Stoljar (1995), Mikkola (2007), Serano (2013, ch. 16).

We now turn to another version of the "meaninglessness" complaint: one that centers on a concern that gender self-determination is circular in a way that renders gender category language *incoherent*. We touched on this version in Section 5.1, and we return to it here.

5.5.1 "Well Then Define 'Woman'"

In "gender critical" rhetoric, many attacks on gender self-determination (and more broadly on trans inclusion) rest on an assumption that any word in good standing ought to admit *definition*, and in particular that advocates of gender self-determination owe the public definitions of "woman" and "man".[23] They then note that we are ill-equipped to provide definitions that meet their standards of adequacy – or at least that we have thus far failed to do so.

We will spare the reader explicit examples, but the general case of this argument usually takes the form of a forced choice among three types of non-trans-exclusionary definitions – one predicated on endorsement of sexist stereotypes (where "woman" applies to those who conform to certain stereotypes of womanly behavior), one predicated on superstitious claims about mysterious essences (where "woman" applies to those who have a womanly "gender identity", akin to an immaterial womanly soul), and one that is circular (where "woman" applies to those who "identify as" women, which presupposes a concept of womanhood to be the object of identification). We are meant to reject these three options on political, conceptual, or metaphysical grounds. Since these are supposedly the only three definitions of "woman" on offer (the critic claims), we are left with no choice but to fall back on a definition of "woman" that centers sexed biology and is largely trans-exclusionary.

Objectors are wrong to claim that any definition of "woman" is necessary. We don't, in general, need to define words in order to be able to use and understand them. We don't, specifically, need a definition of the word "woman" in order to talk sensibly about women or to pursue feminist aims (see Barker, 1997). And while the definitions in dictionaries can help someone grasp an unfamiliar word, they don't offer anything like noncircular necessary and sufficient conditions. (See Chapter 1 of Elbourne (2011) for an accessible demonstration of the difficulties of definition-oriented approaches to meaning and the failings of dictionary definitions, and see Barker (2004) for a brief overview of some common linguistic and philosophical objections to paraphrase-based theories of meaning.)

It's lucky that we don't need a definition, because most of the proposed options are unappealing: there is not much to like about sexist stereotypes, womanly souls, or cissexist understandings of biology. But many versions of the proposal labeled as "circular" are in fact perfectly coherent.

5.5.2 Circular Definitions?

Recall the "admissions policy" we briefly considered in Section 5.1:

SELF-ID: A person is a woman if and only if they *identify as a woman*.

Paraphrasing and precisifying this in light of the ideas developed so far, where F is the gender category associated with womanhood, we might get something like this:

SELF-ID-F: We ought to gender someone as an F if and only if they sincerely express a wish to be gendered as an F.

If we interpret SELF-ID as a claim about how we ought to administer recognized membership in our gender categories, it's perfectly coherent – no more circular than a policy of allowing people into a particular park if and only if they ask to come in.

Someone can accept SELF-ID-F without thinking it's constitutive of the gender category F, and this suffices for the needs of most versions of gender self-determination. If we try to go further, and to make something like SELF-ID constitutive of F, this does introduce a kind of circularity, but even in this case it's not clear that this circularity is problematic. Benignly circular characterizations are routine in other philosophical settings.

Consider, for example, response-dependent accounts of concepts like *red*, or *good* which claim that anyone who possesses the concept C is entitled to believe some version of the following:

> Something is C if and only if ordinary perceivers, operating under favorable conditions, would judge that it is C.[24]

If we wanted, we could fit gender self-determination into this response-dependence template. We can do this even without resorting to the kinds of distinctions we introduced in Section 5.4:[25]

> Someone is a woman if and only if a particular perceiver (the person in question), operating under favorable conditions (which might require them to possess the concept of womanhood and have time to seriously consider their feelings) would judge them to be a woman.

We're not defending a response-dependent account of gender categories. (See Ásta, Ch. 1.2, for arguments that gender category membership lacks other features commonly associated with response-dependence.) Our point is that it's common in the analytic philosophical tradition to posit criteria for category membership that appeal to people's judgments about categorization. Analytic philosophers don't typically consider this kind of move incoherent and have an established toolkit for understanding *why* it isn't incoherent.

5.5.3 The Dispensability of Categories

Demands for noncircular definitions aren't especially compelling: many words don't need (and don't admit of) definition, and philosophers are happy to countenance circular definitions in some contexts. So when it comes to gender categories (like *F* and *M*) and category-associated terms (like "woman" and "man"), why do these demands get so much traction?

One kind of answer is historical and political. Demands for these sorts of definitions, and especially demands to "define woman", have become a major theme of transphobic rhetoric, escaping the darkest "gender critical" corners of Twitter to make their way into such mainstream settings as US Supreme Court confirmation hearings (Weisman, 2022). An organized campaign has turned one putative definition of "woman", "adult human female", into a prominent shibboleth or dog whistle of transphobic politics.[26] And some philosophy papers, for example (Byrne 2020), uncritically adopt this framing.

But what might motivate philosophers, who should know better, to buy into these demands? We suspect that one factor is an assumption that's not about definitions but about the idea that facts about gender category membership must ultimately come down to facts about the other parts of the gender system in the here and now. We'll call this assumption the **Dispensability of Categories**. We can spell it out as follows:[27]

> Whether someone is a woman or a man (or both or neither) is fully determined by facts about their sexed biology, gendered behaviors, the biology-behavior norms, biology norms, and behavior norms they are subject to, and their feels about biology and behavior.

Borrowing a piece of jargon from metaphysicians, the Dispensability of Categories says that gender category membership *supervenes on* these other parts of the gender system: if there are two people, one of whom belongs to a gender category and the other of whom does not, they must differ in their sexed biology, or their gendered behavior, or which norms they are subject to, or the like. The Dispensability of Categories is at odds with the irreducible categories required by many versions of gender self-determination.[28]

Although explicit definitions of "woman" and "man" often presuppose the Dispensability of Categories, it is logically independent of the claim that gender categories can be defined. For example, a believer in the Dispensability of Categories might refuse the demand for explicit necessary and sufficient conditions on womanhood (and manhood and nonbinariness) and instead treat gender categories as *cluster concepts*. They might claim that belonging to a gender category is a matter not of having any particular set of features but of having enough traits in a particular cluster that includes only biology, behavior, biology-feels, practice-feels, and being subject to certain norms.[29] Conversely, someone can reject the Dispensability of Categories while treating SELF-ID as a definition of womanhood.

Why believe in the Dispensability of Categories? Unfortunately, arguments for it are hard to come by; it is typically presupposed rather than explicitly defended. We think one plausible motivation is the lack of an obvious alternative. If gender category membership isn't a matter of biology, gendered behavior, and one's relationship to feels and norms about those things, what exactly are gender categories? And how can we settle questions about the extensions of category-associated terms? In the rest of the chapter, we sketch a positive account, influenced by the analogy of names from Section 4.3.3.1, and drawing on ideas from the work of Theodore Bach and Ásta.

Bach and Ásta don't draw the same distinctions that we've drawn in Section 5.4, so we'll set those aside for now. We'll bring back the distinctions in Section 5.8, when we develop our own theory that aims to combine their insights.

5.6 Gender Categories as Historical Lineages

Like us, Theodore Bach (2012) objects to the Dispensability of Categories. Unlike us, Bach is not an advocate of gender self-determination, and his theory doesn't make much room for it. Nonetheless, we can learn something valuable by considering his work.[30]

Bach's motivations are different from ours, and somewhat at odds with the value of gender self-determination. One of his aims is to explain how gender categories can be *natural kinds* that aid in scientific investigation. For Bach, it is important that someone's gender category membership reliably predicts their other properties, that gender categories figure in scientific explanations, and that the features of women and men (the two genders that Bach is focused on) are self-perpetuating and stable over time.

This project is at odds with gender self-determination, insofar as coercively enforced norms are what make gender category membership predictive, explanatory, and stable. Eliminating these norms is liable to make womanhood, manhood, and non-binariness less useful as scientific concepts but need not make them less useful as concepts, full stop. In Chapter 4, we considered how gender categories, like names, can be valuable for the belonging, continuity, and resonance they offer – none of which require them to be scientifically explanatory.

On to Bach's positive account. His central claim is that to be a woman or a man is to be a member of a historical lineage. To explain what this means, Bach draws on the analogy of Nissan Sentra transmission. "A hunk of steel comes to belong to the historical kind Sentra Transmission if it is a reproduction of a lineage of Sentra Transmissions – if it is sculpted and pounded according to a historically specified Nissan design plan (p. 259)". Similarly, a human counts as a woman if that human is a copy of other women.

A person need not conform to any given gender stereotype in order to count as a woman; rather

> If a particular female has undergone the ontogenetic process through which one exemplifies a participatory relation to a lineage of women, then even if she fails to exemplify any of the properties of women's historical gender role, she is still a woman because she has the right history.
>
> *(p. 261)*

Bach goes on to claim that women have the "function" of conforming to historical gender roles. But this does not mean that every woman *does* conform to historical gender roles or even that she *should* (since the internal rules of the gender system might be overall bad). It just means that gender roles and stereotypes have historically contributed to the stability of the gender system.

Bach's theory allows for the possibility that someone might belong to a gender category without conforming to any of its associated stereotypes. His account also avoids circular definitions since it gives a substantive characterization of gender categories in historical terms rather than in terms of necessary and sufficient conditions. However, it falls short of making enough space for gender self-determination.

This feature of Bach's account stems from his reliance on the concept of reproduction or copying. Bach claims that to count as a woman (or a man) is to be copied from other women (or men), but what does this copying consist of? Bach writes, "The most important and familiar process is differential socialization" (p. 260) and goes on to give examples of differential treatment of boys and girls in early childhood. While he allows that trans people may change gender, he specifies that "individuals cannot simply stipulate their gender status as 'woman' or 'man'" and suggests that many trans men and women are borderline cases of men and women, since "one would need to present the right appearance in order to trigger the reproductive processes that confer membership to the desired gender lineage" (p. 269).

Whatever Bach's model of reproduction, it seems to make someone's womanhood (or manhood) contingent on their being molded in terms of the traits that society deems feminine (or masculine). This sets the genders of trans men and women on precarious footing (as well as potentially the genders of nonconforming cis people). And it doesn't make enough room for Ada, Blaise, and Cass.

If we take Bach's Nissan Sentra analogy seriously, we might begin to wonder whether copying is the best model for understanding what it is to participate in a historical lineage. After all, this year's Nissan Sentra transmissions need not be copies of previous Nissan Sentra transmissions. The Sentra has undergone several redesigns since its introduction in 1982, when it was available with either a 4-speed manual or a 5-speed manual or a 3-speed automatic transmission. In deciding whether a particular vehicle (or vehicle design) is a Nissan Sentra (or a design for one), the single biggest consideration is just the question of whether Nissan says that it is, and what makes a Sentra transmission a Nissan Sentra transmission, as opposed to a Nissan Versa transmission or an off-brand knockoff, is that it stands in the right relation to Nissan Sentras.

What if we followed the Nissan analogy where it leads, and assumed being a woman, a man, or a member of any other gender, has something to do with receiving the right kind of social recognition? This brings us to the next ingredient in our positive account: conferralism.

5.7 Conferralism

Ásta's (2018) conferralist theory draws a direct connection between gender category membership and social recognition. On Ásta's view, being a woman, a man, etc. is a *conferred status*. Belonging to a gender category is a *status*, for Ásta, because it comes with constraints and enablements: your gender category membership influences what spaces you're allowed to enter, what you're expected and allowed to do in those spaces, and how people treat you.

This status is *conferred* because it can be bestowed by someone with the appropriate authority or social standing, merely by their deeming someone or something to have the property. Ásta compares the property of being a strike in baseball and the property of being president-elect: what makes something a strike is that the umpire says it's a strike, and what makes someone president-elect is that the current president declares that they are. *Nissan Sentra* is another good candidate for a conferred status; something counts as a Sentra just in case it is authorized as one by the Nissan corporation. ("Sentra *transmission*" introduces complications that are irrelevant to our main point.)

Similarly, Ásta says, what it takes to be a woman is for someone (or someones) with the appropriate social standing to deem you a woman, with the distinction that womanhood is not *institutionally* regimented in the way that some other properties are, but is administered *communally*, according to the informal pronouncements of people in the community with the social standing to make proclamations.

Ásta's conferralism gives us another way of rejecting the Dispensability of Categories. Ásta claims that all conferred statuses aim to track base properties: an umpire is supposed to call a strike if the ball travels through the strike zone into the catcher's glove without being hit; the vice president is supposed to declare someone the president-elect if they win the majority of electoral votes and not otherwise; and the people conferring membership in the category *woman* are supposed to be tracking base properties which in different contexts may include "role in biological reproduction . . . role in societal organization of various kinds, sexual engagement, bodily presentation, preparation of food at family gatherings, self-identification, and so on". But a conferral that accidentally fails to track the base properties still succeeds in conferring the status. Thus, two people who are alike in their base properties may still differ with respect to whether they are women, since conferrals of womanhood may fail to track the base properties.

This way of denying the Dispensability of Categories doesn't guarantee gender self-determination. It could just as easily leave us at the mercy of arbiters who want categorization to track something irrelevant to our needs and desires (or, indeed, to any other legitimate or even sympathetic goal). If you insist that you're a woman, but the relevant arbiters in your community deny you the status of womanhood because they (rightly or wrongly) think you can't get pregnant, then womanhood is conferred but not in a way that leaves much space for people to determine their own category membership.

So conferralism doesn't guarantee self-determination, but is it compatible with self-determination? We think that, with two slight modifications, it is. First, we'd like to modify Ásta's requirement that conferrals of category membership aim to track some base property or other. We suggest that, while these conferrals can (and frequently do) aim to track some independently specifiable base property, they need not. This move is a departure from Ásta's understanding of conferred properties since she claims that they must always track a base property. But we think it's well-motivated and that a modified version of her framework can still do much of the work she wants it to do.

Ásta already holds that *which* property a conferred status aims to track can change from context to context. One of her candidate base properties is "gender self-identification": thinking of oneself as a member of a gender category or avowing one's own membership in the category. On what we think is the most appealing understanding of this base property, it's not obvious how to specify it independently of the gender category itself.

In other words, we think it's possible for gender category membership (in our terms, this might correspond to really *being a G*, or to *being gendered as a G*, for the appropriate category G) to aim at tracking self-avowed category membership (in our terms, sincerely expressing a view that one *is a G*, that one ought to *be gendered as a G*, or the like). This is compatible with the letter of Ásta's conferralism – there is some base property – but perhaps not with the spirit – the base property can't be specified completely independently of the conferred status.

We also depart from Ásta's assumption that every conferred status must come with nontrivial constraints and enablements – some of the things we call conferred statuses might lack such constraints and enablements or have only trivial ones. If you are invested in an understanding of the word "status" in the spirit of Ásta's, feel free to replace our use of "conferred status" with "conferred property" in what follows. Our main interest is in the "conferred" part.

Although our view departs from Ásta's, it's not as dramatic a departure as it might seem. It doesn't entail that gendering currently tracks avowals of category-feels, only that it could, if we changed the rules by which we confer it. It's compatible with the view that gender category membership counts as a conferred status because, at one time or another, it used to track an independently specifiable base property, such as role in reproduction (although it doesn't require us to adopt this view). And it's compatible with the view that most or all conferred statuses in the actual world have constraints and enablements.

But why make this change at all? We think it offers a better picture not just of the actual world but of the possibilities for a better world. It also has precedent. Recall again our analogy with names: names have most of the hallmarks of conferred statuses: they are bestowed by someone with standing (such as a parent, doctor, midwife, hospital administrator, clergyperson, or judge) who performs an act (such as filling out and signing a birth certificate or issuing a name change order) in the appropriate institutional context. Some names aim to track an independently specifiable base property, like Akan names that track the day the child was born (Agyekum, 2006). But a personal name need not aim to track anything that is specifiable independently of the name; people who call someone "Sam" are often aiming to track whether the name "Sam" has bestowed upon them.

5.8 Putting It Together

Bringing back the distinctions from Section 5.4, we can take a page from Bach's book and say that gender categories like *F* and *M* are historical lineages capable of persisting through significant change. And when it comes to the relationship between these categories and their members, we can take a page from Ásta's book and note that there is a conferred status of being gendered as a member of a category like *F* or *M*.

Similar historical lineages, and associated conferred statuses, include:

- the name *Emily*, and the status of *being named Emily*
- *Wellesley College*, and the status of *being a Wellesley College student*
- *the University of Sussex*, and the status of *being a University of Sussex faculty member*

We can better understand gender categories, and the status or statuses associated with them, by analogy with these traits.

In all of these examples, the historical lineage exists because it is widely socially recognized and not because it is somehow abstracted from properties of people with the status. There is no independently specifiable set of properties belonging to all and only people named Emily, and even if Wellesley College students tend to conform to certain stereotypes, that is neither necessary nor sufficient to make them Wellesley College students. Likewise, being gendered as a member of F or M is not a matter of having some independently specifiable set of traits; we should reject the Dispensability of Categories.

Having a conferred status is also not a matter of being copied from others with that status. In the scenario where the entire Sussex faculty resigns, and the Powers That Be hire an entirely new faculty, the conferred status *Sussex faculty member* may persist even if none of the new faculty have had any contact with the old faculty, and even if their personal histories or hiring are not in any way informed by anything about the old faculty. This is an extreme example, but it points to the possibility that being gendered as a G might not require that one be in any way patterned on people who have been gendered as Gs before.

While all of the historical lineages in our examples correspond to at least one status, it's not clear that any of them correspond to exactly one. The name *Emily* can *appear on a person's legal identity documents*, or it can be *used by friends and associates to refer to that person*. Wellesley College and Sussex University are both institutions where someone can be *a student, faculty,* a *member of staff,* an *alum,* or a *member of the wider university community*. None of these relations clearly enables us to pick out *the* status associated with the historical lineage in question; in some cases, we might want to say that there are multiple statuses, and in others, that there is a single status that is somehow interpreted differently in different contexts. This fits well with our reticence to pronounce on who *really is* an F, an M, etc. Given a gender category *G*, there are multiple relationships that individuals can bear to that gender category, and it's not clear which, if any, corresponds to *really being a G*.

Another important feature of the conferred statuses in our examples is that they are flexible, and criteria for possessing them can change over time. We're familiar with changes in the rules governing who can have which name (a legal jurisdiction can reform its name change process, or its rules about what parents can write on a birth certificate), or who can be a Wellesley student or a Sussex faculty member (a university can change its hiring and admissions processes). Similarly, we can change our rules about who to gender as an *F*, an *M*, and so on, and in doing so, we can enact better policies.[31]

Self-determination is already a part of the admissions policies for the statuses in our examples. One can't be made a Wellesley student or Sussex faculty member against one's will, and while names are typically assigned at birth, many jurisdictions have (and should have) procedures for changing them. People can't opt into or out of these conferred statuses entirely on demand (one needs certain qualifications to work at the University of Sussex, for example), but all of them allow for some amount of individual freedom. And all of them could be configured to allow for complete self-determination: it might be ill-advised to admit anyone to Wellesley who requests it, but it's logically and metaphysically coherent.

Our theory shows how a policy of gender self-determination is logically and metaphysically coherent. It does not address the political question of whether such a policy is good. (We think it is, but we haven't argued for that conclusion in any depth here.) Semantic or analytic exercises in interrogating the true meaning of the words "woman" and "man" – or the true nature of womanhood or manhood – aren't a substitute for engagement with the issue of how these statuses ought to be administered. Answering the political question requires an entirely different practical and theoretical toolbox, one far beyond the scope of this chapter.

To sum up: we understand gender categories as historical lineages, *being gendered* as a relation between a person and a gender category, and *being gendered as a G* (for any given gender category *G*) as a conferred status. Given this understanding, we expect the Dispensability of Categories to be false; that is, we should expect gender category membership *not* to supervene on any combination of sexed biology, gendered behavior, biology-feels, behavior-feels, and norms linking behavioral and biological traits.

Disputes about who is a woman, a man, nonbinary, etc., can often be understood not as theoretical disputes about metaphysics or sociology but as practical disputes about who to admit to gender categories. To understand them in accordance with gender self-determination is to adopt a policy that lets people opt into, or out of, gender categories on request. None of this makes gender categories metaphysically special; they are no more vexing than other examples of conferred statuses that we treat as comprehensible, coherent, and noncircular in everyday life.

5.9 Beyond *F* and *M*

In developing the account of gender categories (and related notions) in this chapter, we focused on examples involving the categories *F* and *M*, loosely associated with the words "woman" and "man". But of course, as nonbinary people, we are acutely aware that these are not the only possibilities. We won't attempt to offer a full account of all the gendered ways that people categorize themselves and each other, but we'd like to close out this chapter by offering a few preliminary thoughts about these new gendered descriptors, and how they fit in with our theory of gender categories.

In some cases, there may be other long-standing, traditionally entrenched gender categories that fit well with our historical account, persisting alongside the lineages *F* and *M*, and subject to their own (changeable) norms. But what if we try to apply this approach to words like "nonbinary", "agender", "bigender", "genderfluid", or "demiboy"? On one level, these can simply be understood as referring to category lineages of more recent vintage, but this fails to capture something important about the relationships among the various lineages and descriptors involved in gender categorization.

Consider "bigender": positing an additional B category alongside F and M seems to miss the point – being bigender is usually described in terms of one's relationship to at least two gender categories. So we can understand "bigender" as ascribing a complex relation to other lineages: a bigender person is, or who ought to be gendered as, or bears some other salient relation to, (at least) two distinct category lineages. The same might be said of words like "genderfluid" (which describes, roughly, having a relationship to established gender categories that shifts over time) and "agender" (which is understood in different ways, most of which involve lacking certain sorts of gender feels and not wishing to be gendered into any established category). In addition to ascribing a relationship to a single established gender category, gender category terms can establish someone's position *with respect to* an established inventory of such categories.

Descriptors like "agender", "bigender", "nonbinary", "demiboy", etc. are, very roughly, attempts to reply to questions like "what is your gender [category]?" in circumstances where any response that begins and ends with pointing to a single established category would be a misrepresentation. Such replies might be relatively straightforward combinatorial exercises like "both of these" or "none of them". But if one finds it especially difficult to understand oneself in terms of the established inventory of gender descriptors, fuzzier or more creative answers may be called for. Brennan (2016), explaining why people may gender-categorize themselves in strange or surprising terms by comparing them to "frost or the Sun or music or the sea or Jupiter or pure darkness", points out the importance of jokes and metaphors.

> [I]f one has a deep-seated desire to be put into a socially constructed category that doesn't exist, one may cope with this by

absurdly declaring that one is now a member of some completely unrelated category. . . . Humans often describe things through comparing them to other things, particularly when the person they're communicating with isn't familiar with the thing they're trying to describe but is familiar with the thing they're comparing it to. For instance, if one is trying to convey one's emotion, one may say "it's a sort of cold anger". One cannot argue with this by pointing out that emotions do not really have temperatures, because it's not supposed to convey that emotions have temperatures, it's supposed to convey that one's anger is in a certain sense similar to coldness.

In Brennan's account, these sorts of gender descriptors can be seen as instances of what Medina (2013) calls *resistant imagination*. We can see this sensibility in Dillon (2007), who claims that their gender is "cactus":

> A while back I complained about wanting to replace my gender with a set of outward-facing spikes . . . actually cactus works way better than male or female as a gender for me. It's a little tongue in cheek, but I mean, *look at this*. Cacti:
>
> - care more about sunlight and water and safety than appearances, but still blossom in (bright pink, for many species) flowers when they feel like it
> - are covered in spines to protect them from being consumed, but need the touch of the animals that know how to interact with them safely
> - won't hurt you if you don't hurt them!

That is, as of 2007, the best reply that Dillon could offer for the question "Are you a man or a woman?", and perhaps for the question "What is your gender [category]?", seems to be "I am a cactus" (in some metaphorical, humorous sense). As a reply, "cactus" might lean more heavily on metaphor and humor than descriptors like "demiboy" and "agender", but this only shows that metaphor and humor are important communicative resources, especially when we find ourselves near the limits of established concepts and vocabulary or discussing emotionally charged topics. This general picture helps us to make sense of the range of idiosyncratic gendered self-categorization seen in some queer communities, including not just metaphor-rich descriptors like "cactus" but also exasperated quasi-answers where one reaches for a gender-salient aspect of one's life like "trans" or "butch" or "queer", offers it as a response, and signals that one has no desire to pursue the matter further.

Sometimes, creative vocabulary catches on. As new descriptors become recognized, they can spawn new historical lineages. "Nonbinary" arguably began as a way of naming a complex relation to F and M categories, like the cases discussed earlier (roughly, as an umbrella term for all possible "neither of the above" options in a forced choice between F and M). But "nonbinary" has since taken on a life of its own. There are stereotypes of nonbinary people and a growing nonbinary community (or constellation of communities) with all the promise and difficulty that comes with community-building. And people who fit within a given umbrella definition of "nonbinary" may nevertheless reject the label for any number of reasons. So in this case, it may make sense to posit an additional category N alongside F and M or at least to entertain the possibility that one is beginning to emerge.

A new theory of these kinds of complex descriptors and emerging lineages would be a valuable project for future philosophical investigation, though a full development of this project lies beyond the scope of this book.

Notes

1 The sorts of criticisms in which we are interested center on policing the boundaries of womanhood while devoting minimal if any attention to other gender categories, but gender self-determination would involve analogous principles for manhood and other gender categories.
2 "Identifying as" is often understood in terms of the fraught notion of "gender identity", which we critiqued in Chapter 2. But there are other possible interpretations that aren't vulnerable to our

critique; in this chapter, we interpret "identifying as" in terms of experiencing or expressing certain category-feels.

3 This line of argument is most common in the popular transphobic discourse, but it has also found its way into the philosophical and other academic literature: see Griffin et al. (2020) and Bogardus (2020) for representative examples.

4 With both names and gender categories, there other normative considerations that may sometimes outweigh the value of self-determination: there are good reasons to think that name signs should not be self-chosen but must be bestowed by a member of the Deaf community, that some gender categories like hijra require a specific cultural affiliation, or that only people with certain types of medical history should be eligible to count as members of the gender category *intersex*.

5 Like a boy named "Sue", a man named "Emily" is unexpected and runs afoul of various stereotypes, but he is not a conceptual or semantic impossibility.

6 The "consensual" in Bornstein's "consensual gender" is not the narrow, legalistic conception of sexual consent criticized by feminist philosophers. Someone can assent to a gender category ascription in a thin sense but fall short of the robust liberation that Bornstein advocates. For example, selecting "female" from a required drop-down menu when the only other option is "male", or acquiescing to "he" pronouns because you're exhausted with correcting people, may count as "consenting" in a narrow sense, but neither seems like an embodiment of Bornstein's ideal. Bornstein moreover encourages people to actively reflect on and make choices about their gendered traits, which doesn't fit well with Pateman's suggestion that consent is always a response to an action someone else has initiated (1980, p. 164). In recent years, understandings of consent have shifted, so that many people understand it as a more two-sided process (for example, see Hugs, 2016). It's also possible that Bornstein's idea is better paraphrased in terms of the other values that feminists have suggested as supplements or replacements for the concept of consent, such as access and autonomy (Fischel, 2019), invitation and gift (Kukla, 2018), mutuality (Chamallas, 1988), or self-making (Alcoff, 2018).

7 We think that various more logically complex first-person claims about category membership should also be respected, although nothing that we do here hinges on this. For example, if at some

point in his coming-out process Blaise sincerely reported that he was either a man or a nonbinary (but was not prepared to say which), the appropriate thing to do at that point would have been to recognize this as true.

8 We are not fully convinced by this line of argument (cf. Kukla & Lance, 2022), but we aren't prepared to dismiss it entirely.

9 This issue could also be addressed by allowing for more reading between the lines. We could, say, adopt a principle of self-determination to involve either explicit avowals of one's category-feels or implicit signaling or demonstration of them.

10 In principle, these might come apart in cases where someone is not fully aware of their own category-feels, but even in such cases, it will ordinarily be very difficult for an outside observer to have good enough evidence of it to trump the presumption of deference to first-person authority.

11 These might come apart in a case where someone is closeted about their gender feels, so that they deliberately claim membership in a category while in some other sense feeling that they are truly a member of another category and wishing they could be recognized as such.

12 If the terms "genderqueer" and "nonbinary" make reference to two distinct categories, we think self-determination applies to both.

13 From a political perspective, this type of approach has some worrying consequences (see the criticisms of Haslanger by Saul (2012), Diaz-Leon (2016), and Jenkins (2016).)

14 The community is always in the process of making a collective decision about whether it recognizes Blaise as a man. By talking about Blaise with certain gendered language we are, in a sense, casting our vote in this decision-making process.

15 This function of gender ascriptions is emphasized by Kukla and Lance (2022) and Dembroff (2017) among others.

16 This is also a kind of attempt to shape the social facts of who is gendered how, but we want to distinguish between the (entangled, often coinciding) roles of a gender ascription as a contribution to the gendering process and as a signal to others regarding what outcome one thinks would be best.

17 They might also have such disagreements, but the resolution of such disagreements would not necessarily produce agreement about "Blaise is a man".

18 Compare Plunkett and Sundell's (2013) concept of a *metalinguistic dispute*, where the parties disagree about what standards they should

adopt for applying a word like "man" and not necessarily about any value-neutral aspect of reality that they are jointly attempting to track with that word.

19 The general value of gender self-determination might not be the only justice consideration in play here. For example, if prevailing gendering practices use gender category ascriptions to communicate genital status, as Bettcher (2009) suggests, then we should thwart this practice on the grounds that it is sexually abusive and a gross violation of privacy.

20 Or, more generally, *terminology* or *vocabulary*. We focus on single-word expressions in our examples, but the language associated with a gender category may include multi-word expressions.

21 The vagueness of "for *F*s" and "for *M*s" is deliberate: the choice of exactly how we precisify it involves a number of theoretical complications, only some of which we'll be discussing.

22 Those rereading this section after reading later parts of the chapter might note that we make extensive use of definition-like paraphrases here, even though we will soon announce our suspicion of definition-based approaches to word meaning. Our response to this worry is that the paraphrases given in this section are intended mainly for illustration and are not meant as proposals for complete general-purpose accounts of the semantics of the words in question but to show how it is formally possible that such words might have meanings along these general lines.

23 This argument is most often seen in the context of efforts to police the boundaries of womanhood, and its advocates devote (at most) minimal attention to other gender categories.

24 Versions of this idea appear in Wright (1993), and Johnston (1992).

25 We could also do this in terms of the distinctions introduced in Section 5.4, building a response-dependent definition of the property of really *being an F*.

26 See Hancox-Li (2019) for a discussion of this slogan and its history, along with a helpful compilation of references.

27 Here we're eliding many of the distinctions we previously introduced, in part because most advocates of Dispensability of Categories would elide such distinctions. In principle, we could consider a version of this assumption concerned with the property of *being an F* separately from one concerned with the semantics of "woman", but we think that most people who embrace Dispensability of Categories would also treat these as equivalent or near-equivalent.

28 It may be that some supervenience assumption along these lines is compatible with gender self-determination. If, for example, one adopts a heterodox understanding of sexed biology that includes every detail of the microscopic configuration of a person's brain, then an individual's category-feels might supervene on their sexed biology in this expansive sense. If there is a version of the Dispensability of Categories assumption that is compatible with gender self-determination, then so much the better for gender self-determination. But we take it that most supporters of Dispensability of Categories have in mind a narrower supervenience base and that they would not be satisfied with this defense of gender self-determination.

29 Cluster theories developed by Stoljar (1995), Hale (1996), Corvino (2000), and Daly (2017) implicitly or explicitly abandon the Dispensability of Categories. These theories include category-feels or sincere self-reports of category-feels alongside biological traits and behaviors in the cluster of traits that determine category membership. Hale describes the relevant trait this way: "Do you feel yourself to be a woman? Then according to this defining characteristic, you are". Corvino refers to it as "self-conception", Stoljar calls it "self-attribution", and Daly says that you can elicit it by asking your students for their pronouns.

30 His theory may even be compatible with ours, if it is a theory about a slightly different subject matter (gender categories as they are in our current unjust society rather than gender categories as they might be in a better possible future.)

31 We can also change our rules about what we expect of the people we gender as Fs and Ms – or to use the terminology from Chapter 3, we can change norms that are about gender categories, just as we might change the requirements that govern Wellesley students or Sussex faculty.

References

Agyekum, K. (2006). The sociolinguistic of Akan personal names. *Nordic Journal of African Studies*, *15*(2), 206–235.

Alcoff, L. M. (2018). *Rape and resistance*. Polity Press.

Ásta. (2018). *Categories we live by: The construction of sex, gender, race, and other social categories*. Oxford University Press.

Bach, T. (2012). Gender is a natural kind with a historical essence. *Ethics, 122*(2), 231–272.

Barker, C. (2004). Paraphrase is not enough. *Theoretical Linguistics, 29*(3), 201–209. https://doi.org/10.1515/thli.29.3.201

Barker, V. (1997). Definition and the question of "woman." *Hypatia, 12*(2), 185–215.

Barnes, E. (2022). Gender without gender identity: The case of cognitive disability. *Mind, 131*, 836–862. https://doi.org/10.1093/mind/fzab086

Bettcher, T. M. (2009). Trans identities and first-person authority. In L. Shrage (Ed.), *You've changed: Sex reassignment and personal identity* (pp. 98–120). Oxford University Press.

Bogardus, T. (2020). Some internal problems with revisionary gender concepts. *Philosophia, 48*(1), 55–75. https://doi.org/10.1007/s11406-019-00107-2

Bornstein, K. (1994). *Gender outlaw*. Routledge.

Brantz, L. (2017). *How to throw a gender reveal party*. www.facebook.com/LorynBrantzBooks/photos/a.689691364404892/1532404176800269/?type=3

Brennan, O. (2016, July 6). Gender is a spectrum and your argument is stupid. *Thing of Things*. https://thingofthings.wordpress.com/2016/07/06/gender-is-a-spectrum-and-your-argument-is-stupid/

Briggs, R. A., & George, B. R. (2019, April 19). Why trans-inclusive language is no threat to cis women. *Aeon Magazine*. https://medium.com/aeon-magazine/why-trans-inclusive-language-is-no-threat-to-cis-women-4e7da603a617

Byrne, A. (2020). Are women adult human females? *Philosophical Studies, 177*(12), 3783–3803. https://doi.org/10.1007/s11098-019-01408-8

Chamallas, M. (1988). Consent, equality, and the legal control of sexual conduct. *Southern California Law Review, 61*, 777–862.

Corvino, J. (2000). Analyzing gender. *Southwest Philosophy Review, 17*(1), 173–180. https://doi.org/10.5840/swphilreview200017120

Daly, H. (2017). Modeling sex/gender. *Think: Philosophy for Everyone, 16*(46), 79–92.

Dembroff, R. (2017). *Categories we (aim to) live by* [PhD Thesis, Princeton University]. http://dataspace.princeton.edu/jspui/handle/88435/dsp014q77fv007

Diaz-Leon, E. (2016). 'Woman' as a politically significant term: A solution to the puzzle. *Hypatia, 31*(2), 245–258.

Dillon, R. E. (2007). *My gender is cactus*. http://rax.livejournal.com/104836.html

Elbourne, P. (2011). *Meaning: A slim guide to semantics*. Oxford University Press.

Feinberg, L. (1998). *Trans liberation: Beyond pink or blue*. Beacon Press.

Finch, S. D. (2015, August 13). Not all transgender people have dysphoria – and here are 6 reasons why that matters. *Everyday Feminism*. https://everydayfeminism.com/2015/08/not-all-trans-folks-dysphoria/

Fischel, J. (2019). *Screw consent: A better politics of sexual justice*. University of California Press.

Freeman, L., & López, S. A. (2018). Sex categorization in medical contexts: A cautionary tale. *Kennedy Institute of Ethics Journal*, *28*(3), 243–280. https://doi.org/10.1353/ken.2018.0017

Gould, L. (1978). *X: A fabulous child's story*. Daughters Publishing Company.

Green, F. J., & Friedman, M. (2013). *Chasing rainbows: Exploring gender fluid parenting practices*. Demeter Press.

Griffin, L., Clyde, K., Byng, R., & Bewley, S. (2020). Sex, gender and gender identity: A re-evaluation of the evidence. *BJPsych Bulletin*, *45*(5), 291–299. https://doi.org/10.1192/bjb.2020.73

Hale, J. (1996). Are lesbians women? *Hypatia*, *11*(2).

Hancox-Li, S. (2019, October 1). Why has transphobia gone mainstream in philosophy? *Contingent*. https://contingentmagazine.org/2019/10/01/transphobia-philosophy/

Haslanger, S. (2012). *Resisting reality*. Oxford University Press.

Hugs, R. (2016, September 5). Consent castle. *Robot Hugs*. www.robot-hugs.com/comic/consent-castle/

Jenkins, K. (2016). Amelioration and inclusion: Gender identity and the concept of woman. *Ethics*, *126*(2), 394–421. https://doi.org/10.1086/683535

Johnston, M. (1992). How to speak of the colors. *Philosophical Studies*, *68*(3), 221–263. https://doi.org/10.1007/bf00694847

Jones, Z. (2013, July 26). If you wear jeans, you're not a woman: Transphobia at women's shelters. *Gender Analysis*. http://genderanalysis.net/articles/if-you-wear-jeans-youre-not-a-woman-transphobia-at-womens-shelters/

Kukla, Q., & Lance, M. (2022). Telling gender: The pragmatics and ethics of gender ascriptions. *Ergo*, *9*.

Kukla, Q. R. (2018). That's what she said: The language of sexual negotiation. *Ethics*, *129*(1), 70–97. https://doi.org/10.1086/698733

Labelle, S. (2018a, February 5). Assigned male [Tumblr]. *Tumblr*. https://assignedmale.tumblr.com/post/170534431132

Labelle, S. (2018b, February 7). Assigned male [Tumblr]. *Tumblr*. https://assignedmale.tumblr.com/post/170612114302

Labelle, S. (2018c, February 12). Assigned male [Tumblr]. *Tumblr*. https://assignedmale.tumblr.com/post/170799455807

Labelle, S. (2018d, February 19). Assigned male [Tumblr]. *Tumblr*. https://assignedmale.tumblr.com/post/171057590302

Labelle, S. (2018e, March 2). Assigned male [Tumblr]. *Tumblr*. https://assignedmale.tumblr.com/post/171450194377

Labelle, S. (2018f, March 12). Assigned male [Tumblr]. *Tumblr*. https://assignedmale.tumblr.com/post/171789518257

Labelle, S. (2018g, March 14). Assigned male [Tumblr]. *Tumblr*. https://assignedmale.tumblr.com/post/171862834052

Medina, J. (2013). *The epistemlology of resistance*. Oxford University Press.

Mikkola, M. (2007). Gender sceptics and feminist politics. *Res Publica*, *13*(4), 361–380. https://doi.org/10.1007/s11158-007-9040-0

Pateman, C. (1980). Women and consent. *Political Theory*, *8*(2), 149–168. https://doi.org/10.1177/009059178000800202

Payton, D. (2022). *Analytic methods in the philosophy of gender*. Unpublished manuscript.

Plunkett, D., & Sundell, T. (2013). Disagreement and the semantics of normative and evaluative terms. *13*(23), 37.

Saul, J. (2012). Politically significant terms and philosophy of language. In S. Crasnow & A. Superson (Eds.), *Out from the shadows: Analytical feminist contributions to traditional philosophy*. Oxford University Press. https://oxford.universitypressscholarship.com/view/10.1093/acprof:oso/9780199855469.001.0001/acprof-9780199855469-chapter-9

Serano, J. (2007). *Whipping girl: A transsexual woman on sexism and the scapegoating of femininity*. Seal Press.

Serano, J. (2013). *Excluded: Making feminist and queer movements more inclusive*. Seal Press.

Spelman, E. V. (1988). *Inessential woman*. Beacon Press. www.google.com/books/edition/Inessential_Woman/ohIY00toUIkC?hl=en

Stoljar, N. (1995). Essence, identity, and the concept of woman. *Philosophical Topics*, *23*, 261–293.

Taylor, V. (2013, May 15). I'm a trans woman and I'm not interested in being one of the "good ones". *Autostraddle*. www.autostraddle.com/im-a-trans-woman-and-im-not-interested-in-being-one-of-the-good-ones-172570/

Weisman, J. (2022, March 23). A demand to define 'woman' injects gender politics into Jackson's confirmation hearings. *The New York Times*. www.nytimes.com/2022/03/23/us/politics/ketanji-brown-jackson-woman-definition.html

6

CONCLUSION

6.1 Gender Is Many Things

We began this book by rejecting the claim that "gender" picks out a single thing. In Chapters 2 and 3, we broke down the concept of "gender" into distinct parts: traits (which we further divided into sexed biology, gendered behavior, and gender categories), feels about traits, and norms connecting traits to each other.

Recall the Problematic Slogans from Chapter 1.

Problematic Slogan 1: Gender is the social interpretation of sex.

Problematic Slogan 2: Gender is an oppressive system that ties certain behaviors and characteristics to sex.

Problematic Slogan 3: Gender is a performance of the role prescribed for one's sex.

Problematic Slogan 4: Sex is *female*, *male*, etc.; gender is *feminine*, *masculine*, etc.

Problematic Slogan 5: Sex is *female*, *male*, etc.; gender is *woman*, *man*, etc.

Problematic Slogan 6: Gender is between your ears, not between your legs.

Problematic Slogan 7: In transsexualism, biological sex conflicts with psychological gender.

DOI: 10.4324/9781003053330-6

Problematic Slogan 8: A person is cisgender if and only if they identify with the gender they were assigned at birth.

Problematic Slogan 9: Gender is an important, deeply felt aspect of the self, which deserves our respect.

We can use what we've learned in the intervening chapters to name the thing or cluster of things that each Problematic Slogan picks out. Some are unambiguous: "gender" refers to norms and their enforcement mechanisms in Problematic Slogan 2, gendered behavior in Problematic Slogan 3, gender categories in Problematic Slogan 5, and gender feels in Problematic Slogans 6–9.

Others are ambiguous in ways that our framework helps to illuminate. In Problematic Slogan 1 ("Gender is the social interpretation of sex"), "gender" might refer to norms involving sexed biology (be they biology norms, biology-category norms, or biology-behavior norms) or it might refer to gendered behaviors, or to gender categories. On the last two of these interpretations, Problematic Slogan 1 is only contingently true: right now, we are sorted into gender categories on the basis of observed or assumed sexed biology, and right now gendered behaviors are regulated by norms linking them to sexed biology, but we could change the system of norms to break these connections. Maybe the resulting categories and behaviors would stop counting as *gendered*, in that case, but they could go on existing. And in Problematic Slogan 4 ("Sex is *female, male*, etc.; gender is *feminine, masculine*, etc."), "gender" might refer either to gendered behaviors or to the norms governing them.

While Problematic Slogans 7 and 8 are all about gender feels, they conflate different kinds of feels, as we argued in Chapter 2. Biology-feels, behavior-feels, and category-feels need not line up into a single, uniform "identity", and no such "identity" is needed to make trans lives legitimate or worthwhile.

To talk about "gender" without clarifying is to invite confusion: between norms that deserve feminist criticism and behaviors or feels that are harmless in themselves, between the biology-feels that motivate medical transition and the behavior-feels that motivate different kinds of dress and behavior, between gender category membership and the biological or behavioral features that are commonly used as a basis for permitting or demanding it.

6.2 Less Essentialism, More Imagination

A lot of discourse about "gender" is essentialist: it treats connections between distinct parts as constitutive of those parts, when in fact they are contingent. Throughout the book, we've seen essentialism manifest itself in a variety of ways. Here are some examples:

- The concept of gender identity assumes that category-feels, biology-feels, and behavior-feels always "match" – so that someone who considers herself a woman will also want breasts, a vulva, etc., and will want to engage in feminine-coded behaviors (Chapter 2).
- Gendered norms treat different traits as linked in normal or default cases, and often encourage us to overlook or punish anyone who furnishes an exception to these norms (Chapter 3).
- Reasonable feminist criticisms of certain norms, like the demand that women wear lipstick, are sometimes overextended to feminine-coded behaviors, like wearing lipstick, because their authors treat gendered behaviors as inseparable from norms that govern them (Chapter 3).
- Dismissals of trans people's biology-feels deny the possibility that a person might care about their body for any reason other than brainwashing by the patriarchy or perverted sexual desire (Chapter 4).
- Dismissals of trans people's behavior-feels often overlook the possibility someone may attach personal significance to a behavior that comes apart from its history, or from their

understanding of (or politics regarding) its general-purpose public significance (Chapter 4).

• Dismissals of trans people's category-feels, as well as many theories of gender categories themselves, assume either that these categories are only good for mediating gender norms or that they are inseparable from particular clusters of traits, failing to entertain the range of possible sources that might imbue gender categories with personal significance (Chapters 4 and 5).

These essentialist patterns of thinking hamper our ability to imagine how things could be different or grasp how reality already differs from our expectations. There are already more things on Earth than are dreamt of in popular culture and philosophy. People are not, and should not be, as uniform as many gender norms demand. Gender feels, gendered behaviors and the reasons behind them are more varied and surprising than we could ever imagine from within an essentialist framework. And things could be different at a societal level: it is within our collective power to challenge gender norms and change the rules for administering membership in gender categories.

Anti-trans arguments often rely on failure of imagination: their proponents are unable or unwilling to imagine the inner or outer features of trans lives, and so deem them impossible. The tools of analytic philosophy (thought experiments, definitions, distinctions) can be to prop up this refusal to imagine, but as we've tried to show in this book, they can also be used to broaden our imaginations and increase our sense of the possibilities available to us.

6.3 Our Values: Variety and Self-Determination

This book has been primarily a work of epistemology, conceptual analysis, and conceptual engineering rather than a work of applied ethics. But we, the authors, are motivated partly by ethical and political commitments. While we haven't explicitly defended those commitments in this book, we've at least shown that it's possible to live them out coherently.

We believe in the value of differences among human beings. Part of what makes people wonderful is that we're not all the same: everyone has their own likes, dislikes, values, and perspectives. To demand that a person's gender feels "align" with one another, with dominant norms, or with the presumed gender feels of a typical person, is to disrespect our individuality and variety as gendered beings. Our arguments against "gender identity", our case for taking gender feels seriously, and our vision for flexible gender categories whose rules change over time, all show that it's possible to embrace a variety of individual relationships to gendered traits, without making one person's relationship into a prescription for others.

We also believe in the value of self-determination. Everyone should by default have the freedom to make decisions about their own gendered traits, whether they are choosing which medical interventions to undergo (or not undergo), deciding which gendered behaviors to engage in, or determining how they'd like others to categorize them. Of course, self-determination requires social scaffolding: medical interventions require doctors who are willing to listen to their patients rather than trying to gatekeep or normalize them; the option to engage in a gendered behavior is less meaningful when it carries the threat of severe social punishment; and consensual gendering requires us to change many of our current social conventions. But we hope we've shown that it's possible to arrange our society in a way that puts these freedoms in reach for more people. (We haven't argued that it's desirable, though that seems obvious to us.)

Our book is not the only, or even the best, proof that it is possible to live out these values. Many trans and queer communities provide a different kind of possibility proof by embodying these values – not always perfectly, but to a large extent.

Among many trans and queer people, consensual gendering is standard practice, varied combinations of traits are embraced and celebrated, and it is considered gauche to claim that anyone "not trans enough" on the basis of their physical appearance or observed gendered behavior. Cultures that value variety and self-determination are already part of our world; they can and should become an even bigger part of it.

6.4 Further Topics for Political Philosophers

We've resolved some metaphysical confusions in order to make conceptual space for certain normative commitments: an ideal of consensual gender, opposition to the coercive enforcement of gender norms, and an insistence on the value of individual differences. While these commitments motivate our approach to trans politics, we have not offered anything like a systematic defense of them; rather, we have provided some conceptual tools for understanding them better.

These political questions deserve investigation in their own right. Why should we have consensual gender? Which gender norms are morally objectionable, and is there a way of rehabilitating any gender norms (perhaps as optional genre constraints) that would make them morally better? When is it reasonable to override the general presumption in favor of taking gender feels seriously? What are the points of connection between our politics of gender and our politics of categories like race and disability?

While we haven't delved into these political questions, we hope we've cleared some useful ground for them by establishing some smaller political points: trans legitimacy does not depend on a unified concept of "gender identity", trans gender-feels should not be treated as automatically suspect, and consensual gender is an ideal that we can coherently aspire to.

INDEX

activism: fat 110; trans 69–71, 74, 78
AFAB (assigned female at birth) see assigned sex
Agyekum, Kofi 161
Alcoff, Linda Martin 168
Allen, Sophie 95
AMAB (assigned male at birth) see assigned sex
Amadiume, Ifi 71
American Cancer Society 94–95
Anderson, Tre'vell 78
Anscombe, G.E.M. 54
Ashley, Florence 52, 100, 104, 127
assigned sex 6, 10, 21–24, 27, 163
Ásta 153, 155, 158–160, 161

Bach, Theodore 155–157, 161
Bakare-Yusuf, Bibi 93
Barker, Chris 151
Barker, Victoria 151
Barnes, Elizabeth 111, 138
Beauvoir, Simone de 107
Bermúdez, Jose Luiz 54
Bettcher, Talia Mae 21, 55, 56, 70, 102, 136–137, 170

Bindel, Julie 82
Blanchard, Ray 100, 108–109, 127
body modification 37, 76, 109–111, 159
Bogardus, Tomas 168
Bornstein, Kate 78, 88, 136–137, 168, 169
Bourget, David 16
brainworms: "all about sex" 106–109; body positivity ("my body is me") 109–111; curing 111; rationality ("above all that") 106–107
Brantz, Loryn 138
Brennan, Ozy 126, 155, 166
Briggs, Ray 117, 150
Brown, Adrienne Marie 107
Brown, Justin T. 17
Burns, Katelyn 9, 52, 56,
burrnesha 35, 52, 69, 139
Byrne, Alex 28, 154,

cactus (gender) 42, 140, 166–167
Campbell, Sue 123
Chalmers, David 16
Chamallas, Martha 168

Chodorow, Nancy 68
cisgender: accidental
    misgendering 162; as the
    perceived default 53, 126;
    suspicions of the motivations
    of trans individuals 13, 111–112;
    women identifying with their
    own oppression 10, 111–112
Clare, Eli 111
communication style see
    gendered traits, gendered
    behavior
conferralism 158–161
consensual gender 45, 137, 168,
    179–180
Cooper, Charlotte 110
Corvino, John 85, 171
Costello, Cary Gabriel 75
Criado Perez, Caroline 73, 95
Cull, Michael J. 86

Daly, Helen L. 68, 85,
Dembroff, Robin 31, 74, 140,
    142–143, 145–147, 169
demiboy 140, 164–166
Diaz-Leon, Esa 143, 145, 147,
    169
Dillon, Rax E. 166
Ditum, Sarah 27
Dutta, Aniruddha 52, 53
dysphoria see gender dysphoria

Earp, Brian 88
Eicher, Joanne B. 52
Elbourne, Paul D. 151
endosex 35, 53
Engdahl, Ulrica 47
epistemic environment 8–12,
    20, 31
epistemic injustice 9, 20

Escalante, Alyson 78
estradiol 37–38
ethical underpinning of the
    project 4–5, 132

fa'afafine 35, 53, 139
fa'atama 35, 53, 139
Fara, Delia Graf 54
Farran, Sue 53
fat see activism, fat
Fausto-Sterling, Anne 75
Feinberg, Leslie 137
femininity as oppressive 17, 42,
    82
Finch, Sam Dylan 49, 138
Firestone, Shulamith 107
Fischel, Joseph J. 168
Freeman, Lauren 52, 150
Fricker, Miranda 9, 20
Friedan, Betty 107
Friedman, Mary 138

gatekeeping 12, 22–23, 44–45,
    48, 65, 68, 72, 76, 179
Gatens, Moira 107
gender: concept not necessary
    30–32; harms of 8–12,
    21–22, 64–68, 78, 94;
    identities interconnected
    with 4, 66; makes experiences
    unintelligible 2, 8–12, 20;
    problematic slogans about
    6–8; proposed definitions
    of 10, 134, 150–153, 155;
    stereotypes 22–29, 45,
    49, 64–79, 119, 134, 151,
    156–158, 168
gender abolitionism 78–86
gender categories: analogous
    to other categories 140;

ascriptions 14–143, 168, 169, 170; avowals 137–139; belonging 121–122; beyond men and women 164–167; circularity objection 132–36, 148, 150–157; continuity over time 122–123; as historical lineage 155–158; non-dispensability of 153–164; ontology of 131–136; personal resonance 123–125; political motivation of analysis 132; self-naming 134–136; terms 136, 143–148

"gender critical": "define woman" challenge 153–155; fears of child grooming 27–29; Reddit 25; see also TERFs, transphobia

gender dysphoria: DSM-5 definition 23, 26; World Professional Association for Transgender Health's Standard of Care 23

gender feels: as an attitude or disposition 37–40; behavior feels 42, 45, 85, 89, 92, 164, 177; biology-feels 45, 155; category-feels 42–43, 48, 93, 115–118, 124; deserve prima facie acceptance 101–105; dismissal of 125–126; higher-order feels 91; importance of self-reports 15, 100–102; moral respect of 102–104; relation to fact or possibility 38–39; subjective nature of 3, 32, 40, 49; usefulness as a concept 50

gender identity: cis origins of the concept 11, 20; essence 29, 131–136; subconscious sex 49; received narrative 19–22; unhelpfulness of 21–30

gender norms: abolition of 78–86; binary axis 74; bindingness 65, 116, 125; definition of 65; enforcement of 67, 70, 74; envisioning societies without 111; as expectations 72–73, 75; historical/anthropological nature of 155–158; linking traits 66–67, 71, 74, 76; medical pathologization of 70; and nonbinary erasure 70, 74; social nature of 123–125

gender self-determination 136–140

genderfluid 35, 75, 140, 164, 165

genderqueer 51, 74, 132, 169

George, B.R. 51, 52, 117, 150

Gilligan, Carol 68

Gills-Peterson, Jill 22

Gould, Lois 138

Gray, Robert 108

Green, Fiona J. 138

Griffin, Lucy 168

Griffiths, Paul E. 33

gynecomastia 17, 70, 92

Hale, Jacob 51, 85, 171

Hancox-Li, S.J.S. 30, 47, 170

Haslanger, Sally 72, 83–84, 95, 145, 150, 169

hermeneutical injustice see epistemic injustice

hijra 35, 52, 53, 139, 168

Holmes, Morgan 53, 75

Hsiao, Timothy 108
Hugs, Robot 168
Human Rights Campaign 51
Human Rights Watch 70

InterACT 53
intersex 53, 70–71, 74–76, 80,
   94, 139, 168
Intersex Initiative 53
Ivey, Rachel 82

James, S.E., et al. 55
Jenkins, Katharine 31, 52, 95, 169
Johnson, Harriet McBryde 111
Johnston, Mark 170
Jones, Zinnia 52, 2013

Khader, Serene J. 71, 81, 83, 114
Kukla, Quill 140, 142, 143, 168,
   169

la Pavona, Katherine 53
Labelle, Sophie 138
Lance, Mark Norris 140, 142,
   143, 169
Lewis, David 54
Lim-Bunnin, Luka Leleiga 53
Littman, Lisa 100, 101
Lloyd, Genevieve 107
López, Saray Ayala 52, 150
Louhiala, P. 70
Lugones, Maria 75, 78

Malena-Weber, Laser 117
man 6, 10, 13, 14, 15, 21, 26, 35,
   37, 38, 41, 42, 43, 51, 52, 55,
   64, 66, 67, 69, 70, 71, 74, 75,
   78, 80, 84, 85, 87, 90, 92, 94,
   95, 100, 132, 139, 140, 144,
   149, 156, 157, 158, 164, 175

McGeer, Victoria 102
McKitrick, Jennifer 25, 26, 85,
McMullin, Dan Taulapapa 53
medical transition 8, 11,12, 17,
   19–28, 44–45, 48, 52, 55,
   69–73, 76, 94, 177, 179
Medina, Jose 9, 20, 166
Mikkola, Mari 16, 52, 88–90, 150
misgendering 86, 90, 126
Moran, Richard 103

Namaste, Viviane 22, 51
names 29, 49, 118–121, 125,
   134, 135, 149, 155, 156, 161,
   163, 168
Narayan, Sasha Karan 104
Narayan, Uma 83
Nguyen, Thi 9, 20
nonbinary 14, 15, 55, 69, 74, 79,
   116, 117, 139, 167

Osworth, A.E. 56
Oyěwùmí, Oyèrónké 93, 95

Pateman, Carole 168
Perez Criado, Caroline 73, 95
Perry, John 54
Plunket, David 169
political philosophy, a research
   program 180
Priest, Maura 52
Prosser, Jay 51

Raymond, Janice 100
Reading, Wiley 26, 51
Reddy, Gayatri 52
Reed, Natalie 29, 39, 47, 49, 90
Reilly-Cooper, Rebecca 28, 79,
   95, 116, 117
Restar, Arjee Javellana 100

Rich, Adrienne 107, 116, 167
Riddell, Carol 100
Robertson Martinez, E. 52
Roelofs, Luke 24, 25
Roman, Amanda 56
Ruddick, Sara 108

Saul, Jennifer 169
Schilt, Kristen 104
Schmidt, Johana 53
Schulz, Sarah L. 22
self-identity see gender self-
    determination
Sequeira, Rovel 52
Serano, Julia 17, 49, 51, 52, 53,
    78–79, 83, 100, 127, 137, 150
sex-gender distinction 4, 6, 7, 14,
    33, 34, 52, 53, 89
sexed biology 33–34
sexism: as the alleged cause of
    gender feels 24, 80, 105,
    111–118, 151; as the origin of
    gender norms 68, 72
Simmons, Treavian 94
Smith, Andrea 71
Sorensen, Roy 54
Spade, Dean 21,22
Spelman, Elizabeth V. 107, 150
St. Croix, Cat 31
Stalnaker, Robert 17
stereotypes see gender;
    transphobia
Stock, Kathleen 26, 28, 89
Stoljar, Natalie 85, 150, 171
Stone, Sandy 21, 51, 100
Sullivan, Andrew 27, 51, 52
Sundell, Tim 169

Taylor, Vivian 138
Temple, Alex 95

TERFs (trans exclusionary
    radical feminists) 23–29, 48,
    78; see also "gender critical",
    transphobia
testosterone 34, 37, 38, 41, 70, 78
Tobia, Jacob 55, 56
tomboy 19, 27
Tomson, Anastacia 22
trans denial/self-doubt 12,
    29–30, 38; "the transgender
    question" 1; unique
    perspective of 11, 13, 40–41,
    109
transfeminine 13, 55, 70, 72, 82,
    100, 105, 108, 109, 112, 114,
    124–125
transmasculine 55, 69, 70, 86,
    100, 105, 157
transphobia: accused of having a
    paraphilia 108–109; accused of
    internalized prejudice 19–20,
    100, 111, 118; accused of
    internet bandwagons 100;
    alliance between conservatives
    and feminists 9–10; conversion
    therapy 49; meaninglessness
    objections 148–150; see
    TERFs, "gender critical"
Twitter 47, 55, 153

Veale, Jaimie F. 104

Weisman, Jonathan 153
Wenner, Danielle M. 52, 14
Westbrook, Laurel 104
Wiepjes, Chantal M. 104
Wilchens, Riki 78
Williams, Cristan 49
Williams, Rachel A. 90
Williamson, Timothy 54

Wilson, Erin C. 104

Wollstonecraft, Mary 107

woman 6, 10, 13, 14, 15, 21, 26, 27, 30, 35, 37, 38, 39, 41, 42, 43, 51, 52, 55, 64, 68, 69, 70, 71, 72, 74, 75, 76, 77, 78, 82, 84, 85, 87, 92, 93, 94, 95, 100, 105, 112, 116, 117, 122, 124, 132, 139, 140, 144, 149, 150–153, 156, 157, 158, 164, 175

World Professional Association for Transgender Health 23

Young, Antonia 52

Printed in Great Britain
by Amazon